REPLACING AMERICA

HOW SOCIALISTS DESTROY DEMOCRACY

BY

GIL VANORDER, JR

COPYRIGHT

REPLACING AMERICA How Socialists Destroy Democracy

By Gil VanOrder, Jr.

Copyright 2020 by Gil VanOrder, Jr.

ISBN: 9798676287788

DEDICATION

This book is dedicated to my five grandchildren, Rachel, Hannah, Sarah, Rebecca, and Matthew.

TABLE OF CONTENTS

PREFACE

Gil VanOrder and I have been close friends for many years. Among our many common interests, we both love to write. Although the subject matter of our writing is usually different, one thing that we are both passionate about is the truth. Gil's latest book, *Replacing America,* certainly is motivated by this passion. In clear and compelling language, it exposes many of the most glaring problems that are undermining the foundations of our country and driving us toward destruction. The identity of these problems is clearly defined in the chapter headings. Unfortunately, the information provided in these pages is not familiar to many Americans, because it is consciously withheld by the mainstream media and the place that should be most concerned with exposing it, our nation's institutions of higher learning.

I believe that those who have received their education in most of our nation's colleges and universities and who receive most of their news via the mainstream media are either not aware of or ignore the dangers posed by the problems presented in this critically important book. This is not only unfortunate, it is extremely dangerous, for the maelstrom that these problems could unleash have the potential to affect everyone, including those who ignore them.

The vital information presented in this book is not specifically directed at either conservatives or liberals, or anyone in between. It is a must read for everyone who is concerned about the state of our nation and hopes to see America once again become the shining city upon a hill that serves as a beacon of light and hope for the entire world.

Steve Bartholomew

CHAPTER 1: ESTABLISHING ECONOMIC JUSTICE

There is a new world coming soon to America. It will arrive shortly after the majority of Americans have accepted what is being taught by educators in today's public-school system, professors in our colleges and universities, mainstream news pundits, liberal politicians, and the endless stream of misinformed charlatans on social media platforms. All these voices have combined in an effort to change American thought. Few stop to ask themselves if these voices are telling the truth. In fact, there is a substantial amount of evidence that indicates that they are not. The purpose of this book is to corroborate this accusation and to demonstrate the ways democracy is being destroyed.

In addition to the aforementioned voices, there are other more sinister voices currently working to sow sophistry in America. These voices come from outside the United States. They are covert operatives involved in trying to create anarchy in the United States, not with the aim of making it better, but with the ultimate aim of replacing American democracy with socialism.

According to FBI reports, Russian and Chinese agents have infiltrated America's universities, corporate boardrooms, scientific labs, social media companies, and political institutions. These foreign agents have successfully engaged in cyber-attacks and computer intrusions including the hacking into the accounts of U.S. officials. A report drafted by

The Central Intelligence Agency (CIA), The Federal Bureau of Investigation (FBI), and The National Security Agency (NSA) reveals direct linkage of Russia to covert efforts to suppress voting and provide illegal campaign financing.[1] The U.S. House of Representatives Permanent Select Committee on Intelligence reported numerous instances of political ads paid for by Russia designed to "sow discord online."[2]

Kremlin's cyber soldiers aren't the only country running disinformation campaigns in the US. In fact, every country that has an adversarial stance with the United States has amassed at least hundreds of online propaganda warriors, mostly in the form of bots and fake accounts. An Oxford study noted at least 25 nations were utilizing them.[3]

According to the nonpartisan Institute for Critical Infrastructure Technology (ICIT), Iran, China, the Muslim Brotherhood, and ISIL's Cyber Caliphate all have "troll armies." The goals for these armies are to infiltrate and disrupt America's intelligence sources, to create discontent and division within America's various population groups (see chapter 4), and to cause the citizenry to distrust America's institutions and leaders.

The most successful foreign agents have been those from socialist countries who endeavor to convince U.S. citizens that capitalism is evil. The propaganda includes teaching that capitalism creates a super-rich class of people (made up primarily of white men) while, at the same time, creates little opportunity for the poor (made up primarily of minorities). Thus, caring individuals come to believe that America's system is both racist and unfair. This belief leads to a desire for a new form of government that provides economic justice through income equality. Many Americans are now convinced that "democratic socialism" will accomplish that goal. Politicians like Bernie Sanders and Alexandria Ocasio-Cortez are convinced it is possible to create such a utopian society even though it has been tried many times without success.

Despite the long history of abject failure by country after country that has tried to implement socialism, idealistic Americans believe that democratic socialism will be different. It will succeed where Communism, Marxism, and other forms of socialism did not. The impossibility of implementing a socialism that is democratic will be examined later in this chapter, but it is important to first review what has resulted in the past by those promising a better society through socialism. Economist Walter Williams aptly stated that "socialists never reveal what turns out to be their true agenda. Look at the kind of statements socialist leaders have used to gain power. Note that all of their slogans before gaining power bore little relation to the facts after they had power."

Vladimir Lenin promised, "Under socialism all will govern in turn and will soon become accustomed to no one governing."

Lenin's successor, Joseph Stalin, said, "Advance towards socialism cannot but cause the exploiting elements to resist the advance, and the resistance of the exploiters cannot but lead to the inevitable sharpening of the class struggle."

Then there's China's Chairman Mao Zedong, who said, "Socialism must be developed in China, and the route toward such an end is a democratic revolution, which will enable socialist and communist consolidation over a length of time. It is also important to unite with the middle peasants, and educate them on the failings of capitalism."

Cuban dictator Fidel Castro said, "Capitalism has neither the capacity, nor the morality, nor the ethics to solve the problems of poverty. We must establish a new world order based on justice, on equity, and on peace." He added, "I find capitalism repugnant. It is filthy, it is gross, it is alienating… because it causes war, hypocrisy and competition."

Venezuelan dictator Hugo Chavez promised, "I am going to do my best to try to create a country in which children are not living in poverty, in which kids can go to college, in which old people have health care." Adding, "I am convinced that the path to a new, better and possible world is not capitalism, the path is socialism."

His successor Nicolas Maduro said, "Fidel Castro represents the dignity of the South American continent against empires. He's a living legend: an icon of independence and freedom across the continent."

What were the results of these "great" socialist leaders' utopian promises?

Lenin's cruel reign as a tyrannical dictator hardly left anyone becoming "accustomed to no one governing."

Stalin's campaign didn't mention that he would enact policies that would lead to the slaughter of 62 million people in the Soviet Union between 1917 to 1987.

Mao didn't mention that his People's Republic of China would engage in brutal acts that would lead to the loss of 76 million lives at the hands of the government from 1949 to 1987.

Castro should have said that *socialism* has neither the capacity, nor the morality, nor the ethics to solve the problems of poverty. His programs totally failed. In Cuba people work for the government and receive $15 a month (doctors receive $18) which barely buys beans and rice and a little cooking oil. Cuba today is an island prison with no escape. People are starving even though their waters are alive with fish, but no fishing boats are allowed since they would be used to escape from "paradise" to the evil United States.

Did the leaders of Venezuela deliver on their promise to create a country in which children are not living in poverty? Just the opposite. Socialist leaders took the richest country in South America and turned it into the poorest. Socialism has turned oil-rich Venezuela into a place where there are shortages of everything from toilet paper to bread, where electricity keeps shutting down, and where there are long lines of people hoping to get food, people complaining that they cannot feed their families. Those who dare to protest against Maduro's failed regime are mercilessly killed.

Because socialism is a fight against basic human nature, it requires brute force in the attempt to reach its goals. The best warning about socialism comes from Aesop, who said, "Those who voluntarily put power into the hands of a tyrant … must not wonder if it be at last turned against themselves."[4]

Democratic Socialism

Ilya Somin points out that the current advocates of "democratic socialism" argue that this awful record isn't relevant to their proposals. They draw an important distinction between their agenda and that of the socialist movements that caused such enormous suffering in other nations. They emphasize that these earlier experiments in socialism were undertaken by authoritarian regimes. By contrast, today's democratic socialists are committed to multi-party democracy. Mistakes and abuses of power will be curbed by electoral competition.

According to advocates of democratic socialism, "If the government abuses its power or mismanages the newly socialized economy, we can just 'vote the bastards out.' Any aspiring American Lenin or Hugo Chavez will be voted out of office or—better still—will never be elected in the first place." Unfortunately, the democratic part of democratic socialism is unlikely to save us from the socialist part. Voters in democratic systems can and do elect dangerous demagogues. Hugo Chavez was democratically elected.

A socialist state that controls the media would make it nearly impossible for voters to acquire enough knowledge to effectively monitor the government. It would greatly exacerbate the already severe problem of voter ignorance that plagues modern democracy. In a world where most voters do not even know basic facts such as being able to name the three branches of the federal government, it is highly unlikely they will learn enough to properly monitor a socialist state. This is especially true if the media only reports news that supports democratic socialist talking points.

For three years the media in American had citizens believing that President Donald Trump had conspired with Russia's President Putin to rig the 2016 election. Some even suggested Trump was a Russian spy. If the media in a democratic country can convince its citizens that a president is corrupt when he is not, that same media can convince the public that a president is not corrupt when he is. Even in a democratic country, the media can use misinformation to fool the public into believing total falsehoods.

It is unlikely anyone will be able to quickly implement the full socialist agenda, or transform the US into another Venezuela. But if left unchecked, the growing acceptance of democratic socialism on the left increases the odds that such things would happen over time.[5] As often stated by economist Dr. Thomas Sowell, "If you give the government enough power to create 'social justice,' you have given it enough power to create despotism."

One of the many things the current crop of democratic socialists fails to understand is that people are basically selfish. If left unchecked, leaders fall prey to the temptations of deceit, greed, and absolute power. Even those who today wish only the best for everyone will become tomorrow's despots when given the power. Socialism itself is rooted in selfishness and envy. The idea that taxpayers owe it to you to pay for what you want creates a self-centered sense of entitlement to what other people have earned. No one is entitled to anything they haven't earned. If they think they are, there is no incentive to earn anything. Why work if the government is going to provide you with all that you are "entitled" to? Such a concept never works. Consider the following example.

The teacher knows best.

A story is told about a group of students who complained about the pressures of competing for good grades. The teacher offered them a solution. He said he was willing to take everyone's test scores, average them, and give everyone the same grade that resulted from that average. The students were more than delighted to accept the teacher's offer. The next marking period, however, the average score was below passing. Every student had failed. Why? Because those who normally studied hard to obtain a good grade now felt it was not necessary because everyone would get the same grade regardless of their effort. There was no incentive to be the best in the class because it would not be reflective of their grade. They would get the same one as the rest of the students.

Those who normally did the least amount of studying now did none at all. They were certain that the efforts of the studious ones would enable them to pass with absolutely no effort on their part. Thus, every student who thought grade sharing would be equitable discovered that is was, but at the cost of not passing the course.

This is always the result of democratic socialism. Socialists of all stripes (including democratic socialists) suppose that the way to end poverty is through income redistribution -- confiscating wealth from the "haves" and handing it to the "have-nots." Such a notion is like believing that removing water from one end of a swimming pool and pouring it in the other will raise the overall water level. Over and over again, that idea has been proven fallacious no matter how large the bucket used to try and make it work. Democratic socialists point out that the class averaging story never actually happened and would not happen in a country under a democratic socialist system. They are, of course, wrong because it has been tried and it resulted in the exact same thing that occurred in the classroom experiment.

Americans have already tried it.

Unknown to the vast majority of those who advocate for democratic socialism is the fact that such a governing policy has already been tried in America. However, America's first democratic socialist experiments did not lead to shared wealth, but pooled poverty.

The Pilgrims started life in the New World with a system of common ownership like the ideal proffered by socialism. The arrangement proved disastrous, however, and had to be scrapped for one which gave these first Americans the right to keep the fruits of their labor – and the incentive to produce more.

The 104 people who arrived at Plymouth Rock on December 21, 1620, were organized under a charter which imposed a seven-year period of joint ownership. Thus, from the day they arrived in the new world, all clothing, houses, lands, crops, and cash were jointly owned. No matter how hard a man might work, he had little hope of personal gain for his effort.

It led to a social order at odds with the dictates of human nature and what historian James Eggleston called a "sinking of personal interest ..., in dissensions and insubordination, in unthrift and famine."

The Pilgrims gathered what Governor Bradford described as a "small harvest" and celebrated their first Thanksgiving with the Indians in the autumn of 1621.

Another small harvest followed in 1622. The meager return came in part because of the lack of personal incentive to overproduce through hard work. Governor Bradford wrote that common ownership "was found to breed much confusion and discontent, and retard much employment which would have been to the general benefit and comfort." Bradford also wrote that the more seasoned and accomplished men took it as an affront to be on par and forced to share in the same labor and rations as the "meaner and younger sort."

The "pinch of hunger" forced the Pilgrims to abandon their corporate charter in March of 1623. After "much debate," Governor Bradford "allowed each man to plant corn for his own particular [for his own household] and to trust themselves for that ... so every family was assigned a parcel of land, according to the proportion of their number ... this was very successful. It made all hands very industrious, so that much more corn was planted than otherwise would have been by any means the governor or any other could devise."

Suddenly, these heretofore mediocre farmers made their own capitalist "great leap forward." Authors D. James Kennedy and Charles Hull Wolfe report that while the Pilgrims planted 26 acres of corn, barley, and peas in 1621, and nearly 60 acres the next year, they planted 184 acres in 1623. Bradford reported that "instead of famine, now God gave them plenty, and the face of things was changed, to the rejoicing of the hearts of many." Under the new system of private enterprise, "any general want or famine hath not been amongst them since to this day."[6]

Socialism sounds great.

Dr. Sowell wrote, "Socialism sounds great. It has always sounded great. And it will probably always continue to sound great. It is only when you go beyond rhetoric, and start looking at the facts, that socialism turns out to be a big disappointment, if not a disaster.

"But people who attribute income inequality to capitalists exploiting workers, as Karl Marx claimed, never seem to get around to testing that belief against facts — such as the fact that none of the Marxist regimes around the world has ever had as high a standard of living for working people as there is in capitalist countries.

"But facts are seldom allowed to contaminate the beautiful vision of the left. What matters to the true believers are the ringing slogans, endlessly repeated. But the very idea of subjecting their pet notions to the test of hard facts will probably not even occur to those who are cheering for socialism and for other bright ideas of the political left."[7]

Sowell also pointed out that, "Under new economic policies beginning in the 1990s, tens of millions of people in India have risen above that country's poverty level. In China, under similar policies begun earlier, a million people a month have risen out of poverty." What were these new economic policies? They were all designed to move toward a more capitalistic system.

Unfortunately, this is not welcomed news by the radical left because these economic policies were evil capitalistic ventures and hence politically incorrect. So, such facts are simply ignored. Sowell quotes French writer Raymond Aron who admits that intellectuals want to see prosperity only "through State intervention" and "the revolutionary code" and hence are resentful over such capitalistic victories. Better poor under socialism than well off under capitalism seems to be their motto!

Jason Mattera makes the observation that, "One of the things the utopians do in order to push their statist society is they have to attack successful people. They have to attack independent, industrious people. Because if they don't, then it disproves their entire enterprise.

Leftists are trying to say that society stinks. You can't succeed in this society. So, you cannot point to successful people, independent people, and industrious people because that shows if you work hard enough, or if you think hard enough, or if you pursue your interests, then you can actually succeed in this society."[8]

This behavior is straight out of Alinsky's *Rules For Radicals*. Alinsky called for radicals to defend their agenda by ridiculing the opposition. "Ridicule is man's most potent weapon. It is almost impossible to counterattack ridicule," Alinsky writes. "Also, it infuriates the opposition, who then react to your advantage." We see this in today's media coverage of conservatives.

Ridicule is much easier to do than to prove how entitlements elevate the poor to prosperity. Giving poor people money never makes them prosperous. Only jobs can do that. The most effective antipoverty program ever devised is a job. America has spent trillions on anti-poverty programs – yet, we still have the poor among us. These programs don't end poverty. They just incentivize it.

Even the poor in America, however, are far better off than the poor in socialist countries.

Poverty in the United States

Here are some facts about persons in America defined as "poor" by the Census Bureau, taken from various government reports prior to the covid-19 pandemic:

- 80 percent of poor households have air conditioning.
- Nearly three-fourths have a car or truck, and 31 percent have two or more cars or trucks.
- Nearly two-thirds have cable or satellite television.
- Half have a personal computer, and one in seven have two or more computers.
- 43 percent have Internet access.
- One-third of poor families with children have a wide-screen plasma or LCD television.
- One-fourth have a digital video recorder system, such as a TiVo.
- More than half of them have a video game system, such as an Xbox or PlayStation.

When you compare this with the poor in any socialist country in the world, you realize that the poor under capitalism are far better off.

Words from the wise

The American dream cannot come true with a government that punishes ambition, creativity, and success while rewarding failure. There is no equality or fairness in forced equal outcomes.

As Abraham Lincoln said of a socialist system, "the Government, which cannot make everyone rich, is trying to accomplish what it can do — make everyone poor."

Thomas Jefferson understood the risk of socialism when he said, "Democracy will cease to exist when you take away from those who are willing to work and give it to those who are not."

Winston Churchill, said this of socialism: "Socialism is a philosophy of failure, the creed of ignorance, and the gospel of envy. Its inherent virtue is the equal sharing of misery."

Jamaica

Let me conclude this chapter with an article by Andrew Scott:

> "Mom, what happened to Sesame Street?" I was an inquisitive six-year old and my little mind could not comprehend why Big Bird, Ernie, the Cookie Monster, and

their beloved stuffed friends had vanished from the only TV station in Jamaica. It was the late 1970s and my dear mother attempted to explain that the government had banned the children's program and other "foreign" programs.

Michael Manley, the nation's prime minister and leader of the People's National Party, had begun implementing socialist policies, actively increasing the government's ownership of private enterprise and regulating the private sector, while strengthening ties with communist Cuba, 90 miles to Jamaica's north. The Caribbean island's experiment with socialism was cut short, however, when massive food shortages – compounded by restrictions on imported goods, a stagnant economy, and widespread discontent – led Jamaicans in 1980 to vote out the socialistleaning government and elect a prime minister, Edward Seaga, who favored private enterprise, deregulation of the economy, and decentralization of government. Some 800 people were killed during that election.

"People here are very individualistic," said former Prime Minister Seaga, on why socialism, which asks that one sacrifice oneself "for the purpose of building the state," did not work in the island nation. Seaga told Jamaica's *Daily Gleaner* newspaper recently that Manley used government hand-outs to entice voters.

"People bought that as what socialism was supposed to be," Seaga said. "Then the harsh part came, the system broke down and shortages were there and all the other factors that made life distressing." That's when people began to understand, he said. Socialist policies helped give Jamaica seven straight years of negative economic growth. All this leads me to this point. As a Jamaican native and now a citizen of America — whose free-market economy and unparalleled prosperity has been envied world over — it is unnerving that America has begun a waltz with an ideology that has a track record of failure. If socialism failed on an island slightly smaller than the state of Connecticut, it will fail on an even larger scale if the government continues to roll out socialist policies for America.

After nearly 100 years, socialism has an unblemished record of failure. Whenever central planning and state control have taken the place of private ownership and market forces, the result has been the same. A descent into poverty.

Socialism's spectacular crash in the fall of the Berlin Wall and the Soviet Union had many thinking that this tragic and bloody experiment was finally over. But it's as if we won the Cold War only to fall prey to the very ideology the war was fought against. Socialism promises a utopia it can never deliver. It impoverishes nations and people (think Cuba where wage earners make on average $17 a month). And at its worst, socialist tyrannies have slaughtered 100 million people in the 20th century alone.

On the other hand, free-market capitalism delivers when hard work and grit is applied. Why, then, exchange it for something less?[9]

CHAPTER 2: ERADICATING TRUTH

Saul Alinsky, a community organizer from Chicago, set down principles for social persuasion in his book, *Rules For Radicals*: *A Pragmatic Primer for Realistic Radicals*, which he dedicated to Lucifer, "the first radical." Alinsky said we need to have a Socialist, Communist revolution. We need to do away with private property, free enterprise, free market, capitalism. But we do it over time, by penetrating every institution and changing their worldview. This plan for radically changing America has, indeed, taken time. It was first implemented decades ago by such groups as the Weather Underground who terrorized the nation by bombing buildings and killing police officers.

Those radicals from the late sixties and early seventies are now teaching the present generation to carry on the fight. Such indoctrination has proven to be extremely successful as a large majority of today's young people have "drunk the Kool-Aid." Few of the current advocates for social change, however, are even cognizant of the movement's past history. Most think they are the first generation to be "woke" enough to demand change. They have little knowledge of how, for many years, both Russia and China have sent infiltrators into our country to instigate violent anarchy to accomplish the goal of tearing down our nation. While modern protestors view themselves as heroes, they are totally unaware that their cause has been, and continues to be, orchestrated by proponents of neoMarxism. As a result, today's activists who believe they have a "righteous" cause are unwittingly being used as pawns to destroy America.

One of the fundamental strategies of the Marxist playbook is to create a coalition of victims and create "offenses" in order to "prove" the oppressors of the victims are capitalists. By doing so, capitalism can be effectively demonized as the source of all suffering and oppression. This is accomplished by revisionist history and the elimination of truth, reason, logic, and context.

Destroying truth

Already society's understanding of truth has been drastically altered. Previous generations held a general belief that truth was something that existed and could be discovered. Today, the phrase "there are no absolutes" has become the accepted norm for many, especially those who have attended secular universities in America. This is ironic, if not comical, because the very statement "there are no absolutes" is stating an absolute. Anytime someone asserts an idea to be categorically true, he is claiming an absolute. Therefore, the statement "there are no absolutes" is by definition false because in order to be true the statement itself would have to be an absolute. In other words, you cannot be *absolutely* sure there are no absolutes.

Nevertheless, the idea that truth is relative has become a popular belief in American culture. Whatever you choose to believe is true is true (at least for you). This idea is being propagated by using an old illustration from India about six blind men and an elephant. The story goes like this:

A group of blind men heard that a strange animal, called an elephant, had been brought to the town, but none of them were aware of its shape and form. Out of curiosity, they said: "We must inspect and know it by touch, of which we are capable". So, they sought it out, and when they found it, they groped about it. The first person, whose hand landed on the trunk, said, "This being is like a thick snake." For another one whose hand reached its ear, it seemed like a kind of fan. As for another person, whose hand was upon its leg, said, the elephant is a pillar like a tree-trunk. The blind man who placed his hand upon its side said the elephant, "is a wall". Another who felt its tail, described it as a rope. The last felt its tusk, stating the elephant is that which is hard, smooth and like a spear.

From this illustration, modern educators make the point that everyone has their opinion as to what the elephant really is, but none of them have the whole truth. Educators then draw a parallel between this illustration and all realities. Reality is based on what the person thinks reality is, but no one has a corner on the real truth. Thus, you cannot be sure anything you believe is absolutely true.

There are several problems with this analogy. One is that by saying there is such a thing as an elephant, one is recognizing that reality does exist. If there is no discernable reality, then one cannot say that what the six men are touching is, indeed, an elephant. Someone must know what an elephant is in order to judge the six men to be incorrect in their view of reality.

Secondly, the illustration assumes that everyone is blind to the reality of an elephant. But what if someone comes along who was not blind and could recognize the elephant to be an elephant? The learned professors might then state that there is no such person. But the statement that everyone is equally blind disproves the theory itself. The theory claims that no one can know reality and yet the learned professor is saying that he knows the reality that all men are blind. Thus, his own statement contradicts the very premise he is espousing.

Furthermore, with enough searching it would seem logical that a person could come to the correct conclusion regarding what an elephant is. It might take a great deal of inquiry, and perhaps the comparing of observations, but it seems within the realm of possibility that eventually someone could put all the information together and correctly describe what an elephant is. Again, to say it is impossible for someone to know reality is to state a reality which denies the very statement itself. You are saying that it is a reality that reality is unknowable. Such a claim is self-defeating and ridiculous.

Finally, if there is a God (and the theory of "no absolutes" assumes there is not), then such a God would be omniscient and know all reality. Furthermore, such a God could convey what is real and what is not. Just as a seeing person could convey to a blind person what an elephant is, so God could communicate to individuals what truth is even if they are all blind. Even better, if there is a God, He could heal blindness enabling people to see for themselves what is true. This is what Christians believe that Christ (the God who became a man) can do for blind people. Thus, for Christians, the elephant illustration looks like the following:

Such a world view, of course, undermines the efforts of those attempting to convince people there are no absolutes. That is why the second fundamental strategy of the Marxist playbook is to undermine Christianity. This will be dealt with in chapter 7. For now, let's examine why it is obvious that there are absolute truths that can be known.

Even from a secular standpoint, the belief that there are no absolute truths does not work in the real world. For example, you may choose to believe you can stand on a railroad track and the oncoming train will not hit you. Just because you believe that to be true does not mean it is. The train will, indeed, hit you regardless of what particular belief system you may hold. To ignore the fact there is an absolute truth (speeding trains kill) and there is falsehood (I can survive even if hit by a speeding train) is to live in unreality and it is dangerous. In order to make sound judgments (e.g., deciding to avoid speeding trains) it is imperative then one knows the difference between what is true and what is false. To say there is no difference is both dishonest and foolish. Thus, in reality, we all accept the existence of absolute truths.

No one questions, for example, the absolute truth that the shortest distance between two points is a straight line. If you don't think this is an absolute, then I will race you from Atlanta, Georgia, to Macon, Georgia, by going south while you go any other way you choose. If you try to get there by going north, east or west, I guarantee you I will be there before you. This will be absolutely true every time. In fact, you probably will never end up in Macon, Georgia, because you will either get lost somewhere before the North Pole or be continually going around the earth in circles. Thus, there are absolute truths that we all accept.

It is also important to realize we accept things to be true even if we do not fully understand them. Those of us living in the real world believe electricity exists, even if we can't fully explain it. It is because we believe in electricity that we avoid sticking our fingers into wall sockets.

Likewise, we believe things exist even if we have never personally seen them. Few people have ever seen a virus, yet we still believe they exist and take precautions to avoid them. If I choose to believe that viruses do not exist because I have never seen one, it does not change the reality of their existence. I can deny reality all I want, but it will not change reality. If I do not believe in the existence of viruses and so take no precautions to avoid them, I not only show my ignorance, but I may ultimately pay the price for my false belief by becoming sick.

Tolerance isn't always a virtue.

With the rejection of absolute truth comes the insistence upon tolerance for everyone's beliefs regardless of what they are. On the surface this seems like the caring thing to do. The problem with this philosophy, however, is that it is not what it appears to be on the surface. Advocating tolerance is a good thing as long as you know what tolerance is and understand that it must be limited.

Tolerance is not the acceptance of everyone's beliefs as equally valid but the acceptance of the right of everyone to believe what they do even though you know they are wrong. In fact, it is only when one is in disagreement with another's view that tolerance is even required. If both parties totally agree, then intolerance never occurs. What is being promoted today, however, is not tolerance, but the total acceptance of whatever ideas others may hold. In addition, anyone not willing to accept this new brand of tolerance is not to be tolerated. Everyone is to be tolerated except those who believe in absolute truth because those people are wrong and cannot be tolerated.

If tolerance means the acceptance of everyone's beliefs and behavior as equally valid, then it is only a matter of time before a society self-destructs. This is, of course, the goal that neo-Marxists seek. Tolerance must have limits. We should not tolerate evil doers. Intolerance of immoral acts such as slavery or genocide is not narrow-mindedness, but responsible behavior. Tolerance for all of mankind's acts including the murder of people of tolerance leads to the end of tolerance itself. Thus, the unlimited tolerance being advocated is self-defeating.

Furthermore, telling someone he is wrong is not an act of intolerance. You can inform others of their misinformation and still be tolerant. Nor does telling them they are wrong demonstrate a lack of compassion. *Not* telling someone he is wrong when to remain silent would result in his harm demonstrates a lack of compassion. Telling someone he is wrong to stand in front of an oncoming train is not an act of intolerance. Only when another person is considered of value does one care enough to point out the person's errors. If the other person is of no consequence, then there is no motivation to correct him or her. A man would have to be a sadist not to warn thirsty people the water they are about to drink is poisonous if he knows it to be true. In this case, ignorance is not bliss but deadly and informing thirsty people of their potentially lethal mistake (due to their ignorance) is not an act of intolerance but an act of compassion. It is incumbent upon those who know the truth to try to educate the ignorant, especially if their ignorance is potentially dangerous.

Today's advocates for democratic socialism are unaware of the fact that their hope for a better world is a false ruse perpetrated by bad actors offering a Trojan horse. Obviously, we cannot know everything about everything, but we cannot afford to be ignorant of the dangers involved with replacing America's democracy with socialism.

The information age

In the early 1980's, I was taking classes from a well-respected school in an attempt to obtain a master's degree. One course dealt with the information explosion taking place. In order to convey just how rapidly knowledge was increasing, the professor stated that in the medical field alone there are 40,000 pages of new material published every day. Then he asked, "How many have read today's publications?" One smart aleck in the back of the room yelled out, "I have one more page to go."

The professor's point was very clear. It was impossible to keep up with the increase in knowledge in one area of study (the medical field) to say nothing of the innumerable other areas of information. The reality is we have an extremely limited amount of knowledge compared to the vast amount that exists and the gap continues to grow exponentially.

If we were to take all of the knowledge contained in the entire universe and represent it by a huge circle, how much space in the circle do you think your amount of knowledge would take up? My knowledge would probably best be represented by just a small dot in the circle. Perhaps your knowledge would be more than mine and would be contained in a small circle. Maybe Einstein's knowledge could be shown as a larger circle, but it would still be relatively small in size compared to the whole circle of universal knowledge.

KNOWLEDGE DIAGRAM

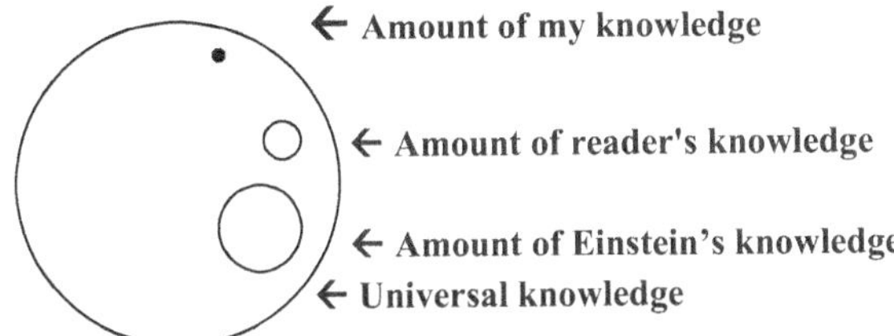

An abundance of ignorance

Because no one knows everything, the honest person is forced to admit there are vast amounts of information, objects, truths, and people totally unknown to him or her. That is not the same, however, as saying that such things cannot be known. These things are unknown because they exist outside a particular individual's sphere of knowledge. They can become known, when they are encountered and become part of one's circle of knowledge. I would like to think that by writing this book those who are attempting to replace America's system of government with democratic socialism will read it and become knowledgeable of the fact that they are being duped into making a terrible mistake.

Ignorance of the truth, however, is not the biggest problem. Far worse, is the rejection of truth. Many people refuse to accept truth, not because they are ignorant of it, but because they don't want to believe it. If the truth destroys what they have been fiercely fighting for, then they will not be open to facts. Present these individuals with all the facts you want, and they will still reject the evidence out of hand. This is because there are two kinds of people (honest and dishonest). An honest person says, "Show me the evidence and I will believe it." The dishonest person says, "I won't believe it regardless of the evidence."

Sometimes the dishonest person is unable to recognize that he or she is being dishonest in what they are saying or doing. In most cases, however, the dishonest person is fully aware that they are being dishonest but are simply unwilling to admit it. Such people may even believe their deceit is justified because they are convinced that their cause is so worthy that dishonesty is okay if it furthers their goals. Muslim extremists, for example, encourage their followers to lie to the infidels to confuse and deceive them. It would be a wonderful world, indeed, if everyone were honest but such is not the case.

Knowledge

Obviously, the amount of knowledge one has in a particular area will depend on the amount of study one has done in the area. For example, a chef who attended a cooking school will know a great deal more about how to properly prepare food than someone who has never learned to cook. A pharmacist will know more about medicine than the average high school student. While knowing how to cook and how to read the labels on pill bottles are important, there are other, even more important things to know. Survival skills, for example, would be one of those things we must learn. We need to know how to obtain food, avoid harm, and stay healthy. Ultimately, each of us must decide what things we believe are important enough to seek more knowledge about. Learning what forms of government work and what forms do not should be a priority for every caring citizen, especially those who think that exchanging American exceptionalism for democratic socialism is a good idea.

If the problem of wrong thinking was due solely to ignorance, the situation could easily be remedied by simply becoming more informed. The problem, however, is much deeper than that. Supporters of democratic socialism believe they have already been educated to the truth about how best the country (and the world) should be governed. While they are correct to say they have been educated, they are incorrect when they believe that their education was being taught by those who know the truth. What they do not realize is the knowledge they have been given is not only one-sided but it is, in many cases, deliberately fraudulent. In the next chapter, it will be shown that deceitful efforts have been undertaken to cultivate socialist thinking through curriculum changes in our public schools. As a result of this "education," it has now become a daunting task to convince the indoctrinated that they have been brainwashed. It is much easier to enlighten someone who is seeking the truth than it is to change the mind of someone who believes they already possess it.

CHAPTER 3: REVISING AMERICA'S HISTORY

Our nation has been the greatest nation in history. Despite its shortfalls, it has always been the country that so many from other countries long to become a part of. It has given freedom and opportunity to multitudes who have come to its shores. It has also done more to assist the needy abroad than any other country in the world. But this is not what neo-Marxists want you to believe. In order to destroy America, its citizens must be taught that the country is evil and has been evil from its inception.

Democratic socialists are often ignorant of America's true history. They have no knowledge of her Christian foundation. Even those who do know their history either believe that America has always been a secular nation or that its Christian heritage is irrelevant. The more sinister Neo-Marxists do not want Americans to believe our country was ever good, so they portray America as fundamentally flawed from its very beginning. To do this they must create a revisionist history of America's founding. For example, those who want to rewrite history allege that the Founding Fathers were a bunch of slave owners. This is allegation is a complete lie. Some Founding Fathers did own slaves, most notably George Washington and Thomas Jefferson, but they were in the minority among the Founders. Most did not own slaves and openly opposed slavery. Many led anti-slavery societies. Those few who did own slaves often acknowledged that slavery had been fastened upon them by the British, and after America finally separated from Great Britain in the American Revolution, many of these Founders freed their slaves. These factual truths about America's history have been replaced with false accusations.

One of the most egregious corruptions of America's history has been the recent Project 1619. This Project was begun after *New York Times* correspondent Nikole Hannah-Jones won the Pulitzer Prize for commentary for an article she published about blacks and the ideal of America. Out of that, the 1619 Project was born. The 1619 Project takes its name from the year of arrival in Virginia of a ship carrying African slaves. An introduction by the editor of the *New York Times Magazine*, Jake Silverstein, explained, "The goal of The 1619 Project is to reframe American history by considering what it would mean to regard 1619 as our nation's birth year. Doing so requires us to place the consequences of slavery and the contributions of black Americans at the very center of the story we tell ourselves about who we are as a country."

Basically, what Project 1619 hopes to accomplish is the defaming of America's great heritage by revisionist history. For example, the Project asserts that the founders declared the colonies' independence of Britain "in order to ensure slavery would continue." This is so absurd it should be laughable, but it is becoming increasingly more accepted as fact by academia. There were many reasons for breaking away from England, but ensuring slavery would continue was not one of them. Not only was England involved in the slave trade itself well before the Colonies (mid 1500's vs. 1619), but there was never a prohibition against slavery given by England prior to the Revolutionary War. In fact, it wasn't until decades after the Declaration of Independence was signed in 1776 that England passed The Slavery Abolition Act in 1833. Even then slavery continued in England. It is absurd to think that anyone in America at that time was worried about England prohibiting slavery. The Boston Tea Party didn't take place to ensure slavery, but because of the tyranny of King George 111 and his taxation without representation.

Several noted historians have harshly criticized The Project for its abundance of historical inaccuracies, mischaracterizations, and absurd claims with zero evidence provided to substantiate them. "So wrong in so many ways," is how Gordon Wood, the Pulitzer Prize-winning historian of the American Revolution characterized the 1619 Project. James McPherson, dean of Civil War historians and another Pulitzer winner, said the *Times* presented a totally "unbalanced, one-sided account" that "left most of the history out." It should be noted that these two men are generally considered to be liberal and not conservative historians.

Historian Allen Guelzo wrote in *City Journal*, "The 1619 Project is not history: it is polemic, born in the imaginations of those whose primary target is capitalism and who hope to tarnish capitalism by associating it with slavery."

Despite all these warnings, The Pulitzer Center on Crisis Reporting, a nonprofit based in Washington, D.C., released lesson plans and reading guides aimed at bringing The 1619 Project into classrooms. The Pulitzer Center's annual report says more than 3,500 classrooms have already used the materials. Plans have also been announced by numerous other schools to include these lesson plans as part of their future curriculums. Random House Children's Books plans to publish four 1619 Project books for young readers—one young adult, one middle-grade, and two picture books.

Re-educating America

Those who wish to replace America understand that the task is more difficult if the nation's citizens are proud of her history and are willing to fight for her survival. Such a mindset must be removed. It is for that reason they falsely claim that all its Founders were racist, bigoted slave-owners, while failing to mention Benjamin Rush, Benjamin Franklin, James Wilson, Samuel Adams, John Adams, and the majority of the other Founders who strongly and actively opposed slavery. President John Quincy Adams said this, "It is among the evils of slavery that it taints the very sources of moral principle. It establishes false estimates of virtue and vice: for what can be more false and heartless than this doctrine which makes the first and holiest rights of humanity to depend upon the color of the skin?"[10] Quotes like this, which were made by many of the Founding Fathers, are hidden from view by the revisionists.

As a result of all these omissions and distortions of history, many have become convinced that America is, and always has been, inherently bad. Young people especially have accepted this revisionist history. It is understandable, then, that they would want to establish a different form of government.

What did U.S. Presidents think of America's heritage?

The second President of the United States, John Adams, stated, "The general principles on which the fathers achieved independence were ... the general principles of Christianity."

Echoing the same sentiment was his son, John Quincy Adams, the nation's 6th President. He said, "The highest, the transcendent glory of the American Revolution was this — it connected, in one indissoluble bond, the principles of civil government with the precepts of Christianity."

Years later, Theodore Roosevelt, our 26th President, reaffirmed this truth when he said, "The teachings of the Bible are so interwoven and entwined with our whole civic and social life that it would be literally ... impossible for us to figure to ourselves what that life would be if these teachings were removed."

Woodrow Wilson, America's 28th President, claimed "America was born a Christian nation. America was born to exemplify that devotion to the elements of righteousness which are derived from the revelations of Holy Scripture."

Similar words were stated by Calvin Coolidge, our 30th President, when he stated, "The foundations of our society and our government rest so much on the teachings of the Bible that it would be difficult to support them if faith in these teachings would cease to be practically universal in our country."

Our 31st President, Herbert Hoover, declared that, "American life is builded, and can alone survive, upon . . . [the] fundamental philosophy announced by the Savior nineteen centuries ago."

"We cannot read the history of our rise and development as a nation without reckoning with the place the Bible has occupied in shaping the advances of the Republic." These were the words of Franklin D. Roosevelt, our 32nd President.

Our 33rd President, Harry Truman said, "The fundamental basis of this nation's laws was given to Moses on the Mount. The fundamental basis of our Bill of Rights comes from the teachings we get from Exodus and Saint Matthew, from Isaiah and Saint Paul…. If we don't have a proper fundamental moral background, we will finally end up with a totalitarian government which does not believe in rights for anybody except the State!"

Are we to assume that all these Presidents were ignorant of America's founding, including those who were there at the time? America began as a Christian nation but has long since left its Christian roots. The consequences of that departure will be discussed in chapter 7. The last thing the Neo-Marxists want, however, is for America to remain a Christian nation. So, in addition to moving the country further and further toward a secular society, they deny the Christian heritage upon which our country was founded in the first place. Are these deniers correct in their claim that America was never a Christian nation, or do our former Presidents have a better understanding of our true heritage? Consider the following facts.

Early Education in America was Christian.

The primary book used in educating students in early America was the *McGuffey Reader*, written by William Holmes McGuffey. In the foreword of *McGuffey's Reader*, 1836, he wrote: "The Christian religion is the religion of our country. From it are derived our prevalent notions of the character of God, the great moral governor of the universe. On its doctrines are founded the peculiarities of our free institutions." *McGuffey's Reader* taught students Christian principles and often quoted Bible verses and passages as part of the lessons. It was used for over 100 years in our public schools, with over 100 million copies sold.

Of the first 108 universities founded in America, 106 were distinctly Christian, including the first, Harvard University, chartered in 1636. In the original Harvard Student Handbook, rule number 1 was that students seeking entrance must know Latin and Greek so that they could study the Scriptures: "Let every student be plainly instructed and earnestly pressed to consider well, the main end of his life and studies, is, to know God and Jesus Christ, which is eternal life, John 17:3; and therefore to lay Jesus Christ as the only foundation for our children to follow the moral principles of the Ten Commandments."

The second successful college of learning, Yale, was established in New Haven, Connecticut. After the charter for the school was granted by the Colonial Assembly, a meeting of those who had petitioned for the school was held at Old Saybrook, Connecticut, November 11, 1701. A decision was made to create a circular for the announcement of the new school. It read in part, "Whereas, it was the glorious public design of our now blessed fathers in their removal from Europe into these parts of America, both to plant, and (under the Divine blessing) to propagate in this wilderness, the blessed Reformed Protestant religion, in the purity of its order and worship, not only to their posterity, but also to the barbarous natives." The circular went on to give rules for the rector of the school. The first rule stated that "The Rector take special care…that the said students be weekly caused to *memoritor* to recite the Assembly's Catechism in Latin; and he shall make, or cause to be made, from time to time, such explanations as may (through the blessing of God) be most conducive to their establishment in the principles of the Christian Protestant religion." The second rule stated, "The Rector shall also cause the Scriptures daily (except on the Sabbath), morning and evening, to be read by the students, at the times of prayer in the school, according to the laudable order and usage of Harvard College."

Thus, America's children learned Christian teachings from the very first year they were in school until their last. That fact alone indicates that early America was a Christian nation. But that is not the only evidence for such a conclusion.

The Declaration of Independence

Even today, almost every student knows that the Declaration of Independence contains the words, "We hold these truths to be self-evident, that all men are created equal, that they are *endowed by their Creator* with certain unalienable Rights, that among these are Life, Liberty and the pursuit of Happiness." Thus, the Declaration recognizes the self-evident truth that the Creator of the universe exists and endows men with certain unalienable rights.

What most students do not know is that half of the signers of the Declaration of Independence (29 of the 56 signers) had been trained in schools whose primary purpose was the preparation of ministers, including John Adams, Samuel Adams, Carter

Braxton, Charles Carroll, William Ellery, Elbridge Gerry, Lyman Hall, John Hancock, Benjamin Harrison, Joseph Hewes, William Hooper, Francis Hopkinson, Thomas Jefferson, Francis Lewis, Philip Livingston, Thomas Lynch, Arthur Middleton, Lewis Morris, Thomas Nelson Jr., William Paca, Robert Treat Paine, Benjamin Rush, James Smith, Richard Stockton, William Williams, James Wilson, John Witherspoon, Oliver Wolcott, and George Wythe. They attended institutions of learning such as Harvard, Yale, William and Mary, Princeton, Cambridge, and Westminster. All of these schools were founded with the expressed purpose of teaching Christian principles.

Those who do not want to believe our nation was founded as a Christian nation point out that the signers had no other options but to attend a college that was designed for ministry education, because almost all the colonial "colleges" had as their primary goal the training of ministers. That argument only goes to further show how pervasive Christianity was during that time. The first institutions of higher learning or colleges were not designed to be secular in nature. They were designed to be Christian. The majority of instructors were ordained ministers.

The Armed Services

The first Congress wanted to ensure that Christian training took place in both the nation's army and navy. In the Articles of War, governing the conduct of the Continental Army (adopted, June 30, 1775; revised, September 20, 1776), Congress devoted three of the four articles in the first section to the religious nurture of the troops. Article 2 "earnestly recommended to all officers and soldiers to attend divine services."

The second article in Rules and Regulations of the Navy, adopted on November 28, 1775, ordered all commanders "to take care, that divine services be performed twice a day on board, and a sermon preached on Sundays."

The first Congress

That same Congress passed numerous resolutions designed to help propagate Christianity among the unconverted Native American populations. In November 1775, Congress provided monies "out of the continental treasury" to the Rev. Samuel Kirkland for the specific purpose of "the propagation of the Gospel among the Indians."[11] In January 1777, Congress gave more money for Kirkland's missionary work among native peoples.[12] In October 1779, Congress once again appropriated funds to expand his missionary work into other tribes.[13] Then in December 1784, Congress announced:

> Congress are highly pleased with the readiness expressed by the Indians to receive a missionary among them; and being desirous to embrace every opportunity of

diffusing the benign precepts of Christianity among those nations . . . [and] hereby authorized to cause a church to be built in place of that which was destroyed during the war, and to engage Mr. Samuel Kirkland as a missionary among the Indians.[14]

In December 1775 a Delaware chief appeared before the Continental Congress. John Hancock, president of Congress, told him, "We are pleased that the Delaware intend to embrace Christianity. We [Congress] will send you, according to your desire, a minister and a schoolmaster to instruct you in the principles of religion and other parts of useful knowledge."[15]

In April 1776, Congress ordered the Commissioners for Indian Affairs to employ "a minister of the Gospel to reside among the Delaware Indians and instruct them in the Christian religion."[16]

In May 1779, George Washington gave a speech to the Delaware Indian chiefs telling them: "You do well to wish to learn our arts and ways of life, and above all the religion of Jesus Christ. These will make you a greater and happier people than you are. Congress will do everything they can to assist you in this wise intention."[17]

In 1788, John Hancock, then serving as governor of Massachusetts, issued an official proclamation to assist "The Society for Propagating the Gospel among the Indians and others in North America" by urging "the good people of this Commonwealth to contribute" for the "purpose of propagating the knowledge of the Gospel among the Indians and others in America."[18]

Most, if not all, of this has been erased from American textbooks. Revisionists have rewritten history to remove the truth about our country's Christian roots.

Historical errors

In their attempts to push the idea that America was not founded as a Christian nation, critics take pride in pointing out some of the historical errors made by those who say it was. For example, proponents of the Christian nation have stated, "The first English language Bible in America was printed by the U.S. Congress." Factually, that is not precisely accurate. But such an inaccuracy in wording does not diminish the fact that the Continental Congress was interested, indeed involved, in making sure that their new immerging nation was adequately supplied with Bibles. The more precise history still makes that clear.

The war with Britain had cut off the supply of Bibles to the colonies, so a committee was formed to address the issue. On September 11, 1777, the Continental Congress reviewed the committee's report, which stated, "...the use of the Bible is so universal, and its importance so great, that the committee refer the above to the consideration of Congress, and if Congress shall not think it expedient to order the importation of types and paper, your committee recommend that Congress will order the Committee of Commerce to import 20,000 Bibles from Holland, Scotland, or elsewhere, into the different ports of the states in the Union." Congress favored the idea of importing 20,000 Bibles, in order to address the short supply.[19]

The Bibles were never imported, however. With the cost of material becoming prohibitive, on January 21, 1781, well-known American printer, Robert Aitken, sent a formal "memorial" or request to Congress for approval to print Bibles in America. The Journals of Congress for September 12, 1782, records on page 469, "Resolved. That the United States in Congress assembled highly approve the pious and laudable undertaking of Mr. Aitkin, as subservient to the interest of religion as well as an influence of the progress of arts in this country and being satisfied from the above report [by the congressional chaplains], they recommend this edition of the Bible to the inhabitants of the United States and hereby authorize him to publish this recommendation." (Spelling has been modernized).[20]

Note that Congress had already authorized Christian chaplains and sought their participation in the congressional proceedings. In this case, it was Rev. Dr. William White of Christ Church (Episcopalian), Philadelphia, and Rev. George Duffield of the Third Presbyterian Church of Philadelphia, who were requested to examine Aitken's work for accuracy. It was only after White and Duffield commended the "great accuracy" of Aitken's work that Congress passed the resolution officially authorizing the first confirmed English language Bible published in North America. So, it is not true that "the first English language Bible in America was printed by the U.S. Congress," but it was authorized to be printed by Congress. Thus, the point remains true that Congress was desirous that the nation not become secular. Congress wanted the people to have access to and to read Bibles in order to remain a Christian nation.

In an effort to suggest a different motive for Congress, skeptics have suggested a number of alternative reasons for Congress's action. One proposal was a profit motive, but no profit was ever attempted to be made by Congress. Another alternative motive that has been suggested was that Congress wanted to show England that the Colonies could compete with the rest of the world in production of goods. These various conjectures are highly unlikely, especially when you consider Congress was not willing to act unless the Bibles were found to be accurate. It seems clear that Congress wanted to be sure that the people were getting a true translation of the Bible so they would be taught and learn the Christian religion accurately. Any attempts to assign a secular motive to Congress's actions are malicious attempts to try and discredit the idea that America was founded as a Christian nation.

Thomas Jefferson

Another attack made on writers who support the truth of America's Christian roots involves Thomas Jefferson. Some of these writers have mistakenly quoted what was alleged to have been written in the front of Jefferson's Bible. The supposed quote reads, "I am a real Christian, that is to say, a disciple of the doctrines of Jesus. I have little doubt that our whole country will soon be rallied to the unity of our Creator." Because this quote has never been validated, naysayers jump to the conclusion that none of the historic facts regarding our nation's Christian founding can be trusted. Such a conclusion is not only unwarranted, but it indicates just how desperate the measures being used are in an effort to portray America's Christian heritage as a mere myth so it can be dispelled.

Just because some writers make a few mistakes about certain historical facts does not warrant the conclusion that they are completely wrong about early America being a Christian nation. That would be like concluding that Germany was never controlled by the Nazis because some historians were inaccurate about some of the atrocities that occurred. The truth about the nation as a whole cannot be discarded simply because a few details have been errantly recorded.

Over and over again, modern secular historians have made the claim that America was not founded as a Christian nation. Perhaps, because many are atheists, they do not want U.S. citizens to think the great success of America can be traced back to its Christian foundation. Such deniers of America's Christian heritage are obligated to ignore a great deal of history.

The Constitution

One of the arguments proffered by such secularists is the fact that the Constitution never mentions Christianity in any of its text. As a result, they conclude that the framers did not want Christianity to be the sole basis for governing. These "experts" claim that the Constitution was designed to recognize and protect the rights of all religions. While that is the current view of the Constitution's intent, it was not the intent of the original framers. How do we know this?

There are numerous ways to determine that the designers of the Constitution were not trying to remove Christianity from its role in American government. One is to recognize that the words in the very first sentence of the preamble are, "in order to form a more perfect union, establish justice…promote the general welfare, and secure the blessing of liberty…" are all the same purposes of the Christian religion practiced at that time. Union, justice, peace, the general welfare, and the blessing of religious liberty were all objects taught in the churches of the land.

A second evidence is the Constitution's recognition of the Christian Sabbath. It is referenced in Article 1, section 7. This section is a directive for the President of the United States regarding the returning of Congressional bills. It is stated in the wording that the President was not to work on Sunday. This practice was mandated by Christian doctrine. Both houses of Congress, the offices of the State, Treasury, War, and Navy department were all closed on Sunday. Even in the civil society at large, all entertainments, exhibitions, reviews, or other things calculated to disturb the religious observance of this day were prohibited by law. There were no laws protecting the observances of any other religion.

A third evidence is that oaths are required by the Constitution. Oath's were appeals to the Supreme Being that what is said was the absolute truth. Prior to its ratification, several of the State conventions wanted a religious test included in the oaths. Their concern was that pagans or Mohammedans might be chosen to serve in the government. In North Carolina, Mr. Iredell said, "It was never to be supposed that the people of America will trust their dearest interest to persons who have no religion at all, or a religion materially different from their own." In other words, the people would only accept Christians as their governmental leaders.

It was eventually decided that such an oath was unnecessary, because the majority of voters would see to it that only Christians would be elected. During the Massachusetts ratification convention debates held on January 23, 1788, Theophilus Parsons, who later became the country's ChiefJustice, made the following argument:

It has been objected, that the Constitution provides no religious test by oath, and we may have in power unprincipled men, atheists and pagans. No man can wish more ardently than I do, that all our public offices may be filled by men who fear God and hate wickedness; but it must remain with the electors to give the government this security – an oath will not do it. Will an unprincipled man be entangled by an oath? Will an atheist or a pagan dread the vengeance of the Christian God, a being in his opinion the creature of fancy and credulity?[21]

Thus, the reason for the absence of an oath to believe in the Christian religion was due to the belief it would not accomplish its purpose. The absence was not, as modern-day interpreters would have you believe, due to the framers' desire to avoid making belief in Christianity a requirement for public office. They did, indeed, believe the country's leaders should be moral Christians. What they didn't want was any particular denomination or practice of the Christian religion to rule and exclude other denominations or practices of Christianity. That was the original intent of the establishment clause prohibiting Congress from creating one form of State Church. It was never intended to mean the State cannot endorse the Christian religion in any way. That is evidenced by the fact the government at that time did exactly that.

The States

Perhaps, the most convincing reason to reject the idea that the framers deliberately removed the word "Christian" from the Constitution is found in the way it was adopted. Every State held conventions to either accept or reject the proposed Federal Constitution. Without exception, all the State constitutions incorporated doctrines of Christianity. Because the representatives desired such doctrines in their respective State Constitutions, it seems highly unlikely that they would vote for a National Constitution that rejected such doctrines.

Below are just a few examples of the wording placed in various State Constitutions:

In 1776, North Carolina's Constitution declared, "That no person who should deny the being of a God, or the truth of the Protestant religion, or the divine authority of either the Old or New Testaments…should be capable of holding any office or place of trust in the civil government of this State."

That same year, Maryland formed its Constitution with similar requirements. Article XXXV states, "That no other qualification ought to be required on admission to any office…than such oath of support and fidelity to this State…and a declaration of belief in the Christian religion."

Adopted in 1778, South Carolina's Constitution stated that, "The Christian Protestant religion shall be deemed, and is hereby constituted and declared to be, the established religion of the State."

A year earlier, in 1777, Georgia's Constitution required that "all members of the Legislature shall be of the Protestant religion."

In 1780, Massachusetts inserted the following into their State Constitution: "…every person chosen governor, lieutenant-governor, senator, or representative, and accepting the trust, shall subscribe a solemn profession that he believes in the Christian Religion and has a firm persuasion of its truth."

Article 22 of Delaware's first constitution reads, "Every person who shall be chosen a member of either house, or appointed to any office or place of trust, before taking his seat, or entering upon the execution of his office, shall take the following oath, or affirmation, if conscientiously scrupulous of taking an oath…And also make and subscribe the following declaration, to wit:

" I, A B. do profess faith in God the Father, and in Jesus Christ His only Son, and in the Holy Ghost, one God, blessed for evermore; and I do acknowledge the holy scriptures of the Old and New Testament to be given by divine inspiration."

If the framers had designed the Federal Constitution with the intention of prohibiting the Government from endorsing the Christian religion, then none of the States would have ratified it. To teach otherwise is to ignore the obvious.

Despite all the evidence to the contrary, many Constitutional "scholars" today proclaim that early

America was secular. They have the audacity to think they know the history of the Nation's founding far better than those who actually wrote the history. Daniel Webster, for example, is far more qualified to judge the nature of early America than any modern-day educator.

On December 22, 1820, as the keynote speaker at a celebration of the 200th year anniversary of the Pilgrim landing at Plymouth Rock, Daniel Webster declared:

> Whatever makes men good Christians, makes them good citizens...let us not forget the religious character of our origin. Our fathers were brought hither by their high veneration for the Christian religion. They journeyed by its light, and labored in its hope. They sought to incorporate its principles with the elements of their society, and to diffuse its influence through all their institutions, civil, political, or literary.

Later in his life, Webster told the Supreme Court, "There is nothing we look for with more certainty than this general principle, that Christianity is part of the law of the land...all proclaim that...general, tolerant Christianity, is the law of the land."[22]

Don't believe Webster.

If you want Americans to reject their present form of government and accept a socialist one, you have to convince them that patriots like Webster were wrong and that the United States was never a Godly nation even from the start. What better way is there to accomplish that than to take over the nation's educational system. Sadly, this has already been accomplished, as evidenced by the revisionist history being taught at every level of our schools. Additional evidence for this takeover can be found in the fact that there has been a steady increase in the number of secular progressive professors (liberals) hired by our nation's colleges and universities. At the same time, there has been a drastic decline in the number of traditionalist professors (conservatives) being hired. Currently, there are far more liberal professors who deride America than there are conservative ones who encourage students to be proud of America.

The Carnegie Foundation conducted a faculty survey in 1999 and found that a mere 12% of professors were conservatives.[23] Mitchell Langbert, an associate professor at Brooklyn College, reviewed the party affiliations of 8,688 tenure-track, Ph.D.-holding professors at 51 of the top 60 liberal arts colleges listed in U.S. News and World Report's 2017 rankings. Of those faculty members registered as either a Republican or a Democrat, there were 10.4 times as many Democrats as Republicans. Langbert wrote in an article published by the National Association of Scholars, "Indeed, faculty political affiliations at 39 percent of the

colleges in my sample are Republican free —
having zero Republicans."

According to a study on faculty party affiliation
by the National Association of Scholars, the ratio of
Democrats to Republicans at Williams College is
132:1; at Swarthmore it is 120:1; and at Bryn Mawr
it is 72:0. In addition, liberal professors discriminate
against conservatives in their hiring practices. Few
would openly admit it but there is evidence to show
that preference is given to colleagues viewed as
progressive. In rare instances, such practices are
openly admitted to. In *Compromising Scholarship*, a
2011 book by sociologist George Yancey, some
30% of sociologists acknowledged that they would
be less likely to hire a job applicant if they knew he
was a Republican. Yancey further discovered that
15% of political scientists and 24% of philosophy
professors would discriminate against Republican
job applicants.

In addition to being discriminated against
through the academic community's hiring practices,
conservatives can no longer safely speak on college
campuses. Students will protest against any
proposed speaker who is a conservative. If their
protests are not successful in stopping the speaker
from coming to the campus, students will disrupt
the event by shouting down all conservative voices.
Rather than being open to honest debate, these
radical students refuse to allow opposing views to
even be heard. Additionally, conservative students
are afraid to speak up for fear of being attacked by
fellow students or of receiving a grade from a

liberal professor that is not reflective of their study (See chapter 5).

Conservative voices must be silenced.

Conservatives are also discriminated against by the major social media platforms. It has been discovered that conservative voices are repeatedly removed from these platforms on the pretext that they violate the company's standards. In most cases, what is really being censored is simply statements of truth that do not promote liberal agendas. In the meantime, these same social media companies allow hate-filled rants by anyone opposed to America, including Muslim extremists. This phenomenon will be discussed in more detail in chapter five.

Those who seek to replace America's capitalism with Marxist's socialism are also aided in their efforts by pundits in the mainstream media who consistently portray conservatives (those who view America's past and present as exceptional) in a negative light. All three of the major TV networks have been found to report almost exclusively negatively about conservatives.

According to a 2017 study done by the Pew Research Center's Journalism Project, only five percent of news reports on President Trump (a capitalist conservative) were positive. A year later, in 2018, Media Research Center conducted a study and found that the reports on the President by ABC, CBS, and NBC were 91 percent negative. A study from Harvard's widely respected Shorenstein Center on Media Politics and Public Policy, reported that at CNN and NBC, 93 percent of the stories were negative in tone toward Trump. CBS wasn't far behind, at 91 percent negative. Then there was the New York Times (87 percent) and Washington Post (83 percent). Media Research Center continues to analyze the news coverage of President Trump. In 2019, it was discovered that the negative reporting had risen to 96%. Other reports indicate that positive accounts of the President are often never aired or are misrepresented. The list of accomplishments in the first three years of the Trump administration is larger than any other President in history. Given the size of the list, it appears there would be a tremendous number of news items to report on. Very few of these accomplishments, however, have ever been mentioned even once on any of the major news networks. The small number that have been mentioned have been given scant coverage.

Often what is given major air time are distortions and out-right lies. In Chapter One it was pointed out that for three years the media spread the lie that Trump colluded with Russia prior to the 2016 election. Worse yet, the major news networks have neglected to investigate (to say nothing about reporting on) the biggest scandal in American history. Federal indictments will soon be handed down for members of President Barrack Obama's staff who attempted a coup to remove President Trump from office. This was done by using what has been called the "Steele Dossier" to get a FISA warrant from a federal court to spy on U.S. citizens simply because they were involved with Trump.

The ultimate goal was to find some evidence that would justify taking the presidency away from Trump. With the warrant, those attempting the coup were able to get subpoenas that required associates of Trump to testify to anything they knew that would be damning to Trump. When nothing was garnered from this effort, they were forced to conclude that Trump had not colluded with the Russians.

What is shocking is that those conspiring to take down the President were fully aware that the dossier was fraudulent, but they used it anyway. Apparently, they believed that deceiving a FISA court into issuing illegal subpoenas was justified simply because they didn't want Trump to be President. All this has been known for some time now, but it would never have become known if Americans had relied on reporters from the mainstream media to inform them because, they didn't.

Liberal reporting

This is understandable when you consider that the vast majority of journalists today are also liberal. This has been shown to be true in multiple research studies conducted over the past few years. In 2013, Indiana University journalism professors David H. Weaver and G. Cleveland Wilhoit interviewed 1,080 journalists. They found that 28.1% of reporters in the United States identified themselves as Democrats, and only 7.1% identified as Republicans. Half (50.2%) identified themselves as Independents. Not only were there more Democrats but more claimed to be liberal and were less religious than the public at large.

Even among financial journalists, traditionally thought to be primarily conservative, it was revealed that 58.47% were identified as liberal, while only 4.4% identified as conservative. This study was conducted in 2018 by Arizona State University and Texas A&M, surveying 462 financial journalists. The results showed that there were thirteen times more liberal journalists than conservative ones.

In 2007, the Pew Research Center found that only 8% of journalists at national publications reported attending a weekly church service. This gives evidence of their liberal leaning, as the Pew Research Center also found that only 15% of liberals attend church at least once a week. That compared to 50% of conservatives who do. If the number of journalists were equally divided between liberals and conservatives then half of them would attend church services. But the percentage of journalists who weekly attend church is even lower than the percentage of liberals in the general population.

Money talks.

The Center for Public Integrity (CPI) identified 430 individuals working in journalism who contributed to the 2016 Presidential race between January 2015 and August 2016. Of the $396,000 that they contributed, 96 percent ($382,000) went to candidate Clinton, and 4 percent (about $14,000) went to Trump, this despite the prohibitions placed by many of the major news organizations against any campaign financing by reporters of political figures.

Anyone who thinks members of the mainstream media are fair and balanced in their reporting is either biased in the same way or has been living under a rock for the past few years. The most disturbing aspect of this situation is that it leads away from democracy and towards tyranny. It is in communist controlled countries that news is all onesided. Consider Pravda, for example, in the Soviet Union. Pravda (which, ironically, means "Truth") only printed news (propaganda) that supported the communist regime. It also printed distortions and out-right lies about any who did not follow the party line. This is what is happening in America today. Honest reporting about conservatives and their ideas has been replaced with "fake news."

There is a war going on.

There is an informational war going on in America today between liberals and conservatives. Presently, liberals appear to be winning the war as a result of the media's liberal bias, the large number of liberal politicians, and the skewed number of liberal professors teaching in our nation's schools. The idea that liberal professors would extol the virtues of socialism is particularly ironic, given the fact that these same professors don't believe there are any absolute truths. Yet, they boldly assert their views as if their ideas cannot be questioned. Nor are they cognizant of the fact that they are free to express their anti-government views only because they live in a free country like America.

In socialist countries, those who attempt to challenge any of the positions held by those in power are met with exile, imprisonment, or being run over by tanks. Similarly, in America today, those who challenge any part of the liberal agenda are publicly ridiculed, silenced, and even physically assaulted by radicals from the neo-Marxist movement. Imagine what will occur if these radicals are elected to power.

Who should lead?

Liberals are more prone to make threats toward and even attack their opposition. This is indicated by the disproportionate number of liberals who publicly accost conservatives while they are dining out, attending events, or even at their homes. It is rare, if ever, that a conservative is guilty of such hostile behavior. What is certain is that such behavior by a conservative would be widely reported by the liberal news networks if such behavior did occur. Yet, you do not find such reports. What you also do not find in the mainstream media are reports of liberals conducting themselves in such a fashion, but for a very different reason. Even though there have been numerous incidents by liberals, these are not reported because the media doesn't want to paint liberals in a bad light. Bad behaviors by conservatives are not reported because there are few to report. By contrast, the multiple bad behaviors by liberals are not reported because they are covered up.

In addition, liberals, unlike conservatives, make statements wishing that harm comes to their opponents including their deaths. One liberal was heard wishing that someone would stab Republican leader Mitch McConnel through the heart. Other liberals have suggested that people try to spread the COVID-19 virus in large gatherings of conservatives. These kinds of sentiments are not unusual for liberals, but they are unusual for conservatives.

Finally, liberals are far more willing to use actual violence in their tactics, as indicated by the higher number of assaults perpetrated against conservatives by liberals than the reverse. Witness the number of liberal assaults on police officers. Liberal speakers are not attacked on college campus by groups of conservative students. On the other hand, liberal students attack conservative speakers on a regular basis. This difference in the amount of violence undertaken by liberals versus conservatives is also evidenced by the behavior of the various groups they organize. Liberal groups are more often guilty of mob rioting, destroying private property, and committing acts of brutality toward fellow human beings than are conservative groups (e.g., the Tea Party versus Antifa).

All of this is to say, it seems far better to entrust a country's leadership to conservatives rather than to radical liberals. If liberals are far more prone to violence, it would seem prudent not to put them in a position of power where they can unleash violence on any citizens who do not toe the party line. Those advocating violent anarchy cannot guarantee what their proposed new government would be like if it is to be run by the same violent anarchists.

George McGovern declared that virtually "every educated person I encounter in the world is a liberal." The truth is, conservatives actually know more than their leftist counterparts.[24] The mirage of liberal intelligence is magnified by their dominance in universities and media outlets, but authoritative studies show that conservatives are actually better informed, more knowledgeable, and better educated than liberals.[25] In politics, conservatives know far more about their congressional representatives, candidates for office, and ballot issues, than liberals.[26] One can only hope and pray that the more informed conservatives outnumber the less informed liberals when it comes to electing our nation's future leaders.

CHAPTER 4: DIVIDING THE COUNTRY BY RACE

There is no question in the minds of most Americans that slavery is an ugly and evil practice. Most Americans wish that none of our early Founding Fathers had owned slaves. We regret that anyone in our nation would be so cruel. That antislavery and anti-racist attitude is not the attitude that the radical left believes is found in the hearts of most Americans. Groups like "Black Lives Matter" have brainwashed more and more Americans into believing that, even today, all white people are racists. The primary evidence proffered for this belief is the existence of the Ku Klux Klan (KKK) and a small handful of police officers who treat black suspects differently than they do white suspects. So, how well does this evidence for universal white racism hold up?

According to the Anti-Defamation League, despite a persistent ability to attract media attention, organized Ku Klux Klan groups are actually continuing a long-term trend of decline. They remain a collection of mostly small, disjointed groups that continually change in name and leadership. Down from a year ago, there are currently just over thirty active Klan groups in the United States, most of them very small. Klan groups that have completely disbanded include the Aryan Nations Knights of the Ku Klux Klan, the Eastern White Knights of the Ku Klux Klan, and the United Dixie White Knights. While a few longstanding

Klan groups still exist, they continue to fade away as fewer and fewer Americans believe in White supremacy. Today, only about 3,000 Klan members remain. They no longer have the numbers or the power to threaten black communities as they did decades earlier. If all white people are racists, groups like the KKK would continue to grow in numbers along with the population rather than decline.

The argument that all white people are racists cannot be shown to be true by the existence of the KKK, because its decline would actually evidence the opposite. Additional supposed evidence for the belief that all white people are racists is the fact that a small handful of white police officers treat black suspects differently than they do white suspects, but such occurrences are rare, even though they get immediate and lengthy coverage by the media. In addition, there is no evidence to suggest that white police officers treat black suspects any more harshly than black police officers do. In fact, there is evidence that white officers are more restrained in their treatment of black suspects. A 2015 Justice Department analysis of the Philadelphia Police Department determined that white police officers were less likely than black or Hispanic officers to shoot unarmed black suspects. Research by Harvard economist Roland G. Fryer Jr. found no evidence of racial discrimination in shootings by white police officers. Any evidence to the contrary fails to take into account crime rates and civilian behavior before and during interactions with police.

In 2019 police officers fatally shot 1,004 people, most of whom were armed or otherwise dangerous. African-Americans were about a quarter of those killed (235).[27] That share of black victims is less than what the black crime rate would predict, since police shootings are a function of how often officers encounter armed and violent suspects. In 2018, according to the FBI's Uniform Crime Reporting (UCR) Program, Black or African-Americans committed 54.9% of known homicides in the U.S. and committed over 50% of the robberies, though they only make up 13% of the total U.S. population. Thus, because there are more of these kinds of crimes committed by black Americans than by white Americans, there is a disproportionate number of blacks killed by police officers as they deal with the larger number of criminals. Theories abound as to the cause for the large number of blacks involved in these types of crimes including poverty, the lack of fathers in black families, the scarcity of job opportunities, gang involvement, poor educational systems, or a combination of all of these. There is no consensus of opinion.

It is not the intent of this book to judge or speculate on the reason for the disparity, but to simply state the facts. What *is* intended is to point out that there is little basis for concluding that there is systemic racism in the nation's police forces simply because more blacks are fatally shot by police than are whites. The reason for the difference can justifiably be explained by the difference in the sheer number of encounters. Nor should the racist acts of a few bad cops justify the beating, stabbing, shooting, and murdering of every person in a police uniform. Many of these officers are also black with children who are black. Thus, demonstrators who claim they believe that all "Black Lives Matter" are phony because black lives don't matter to them if they are dressed in blue.

So, neither the minute number of white police officers who treat blacks differently than they do whites nor the shrinking remnant of the KKK is sufficient evidence for concluding all whites are racists.

On the other hand, there is an abundance of evidence indicating that all whites are *not* racists.

1. From the very Foundation of America, there were whites who opposed slavery.

2. Many whites risked much in their support of the abolitionist movement.

3. During the civil war over 350,000 members of the Union army, most of them white men sacrificed their lives in the effort to put an end to slavery. That is to say nothing of the number who lost arms and legs in that effort.

4. More recently whites joined blacks to march against the discrimination of blacks. Why would racists risk bodily harm to do that?

5. Whites assisted blacks during the boycotts that were undertaken providing transportation for those blacks who refused to ride segregated buses.

6. After the assassination of Martin Luther King, Jr., whites commemorated him by designating a holiday set aside in his honor. He is the only American who still has a day named specifically for him.

7. Whites twice elected a black President to govern the country. If all whites are racists how do you explain that?

8. All across the nation, black politicians have been voted into office with the help of white voters. If these whites are racists, they aren't very good at it.

9. White men marry black women and white women marry black men. Why would racists do that?

10. Every day in America there are whites assisting blacks in need, befriending blacks, and joining hands with blacks to accomplish things that neither race could accomplish alone. Are all these whites to be despised as racists for such behavior?

Despite all of this evidence to the contrary, radical leftists have nevertheless successfully convinced a large segment of the population that whites are not only racists, but that they want to maintain white supremacy throughout America. The goal in telling this lie is to divide and, ultimately, destroy America.

Dividing the country politically

In addition to racial division, the country is also becoming more politically divided as a result of the efforts of the radical left. There has always been a difference in policies between Democrats and Republicans. Candidates from the two parties traditionally debated each other, and then voters decided whom they wanted in office. When a President of one party was replaced by a newly elected President from the other party, it was standard procedure for there to be a peaceful transition of power. Those elected to Congress were expected to work across party lines to create laws that would benefit all Americans, even if it meant compromising by both sides. After agreements were reached and bills were passed, members from both parties often celebrated together over a meal or a beer at a local tavern. Strong and lasting friendships between opposing party members were commonplace. All this has changed. Congeniality has, for the most part, been replaced by rancor, or worse.

Today, it is a rare occasion when Democrats and Republicans are able to work together to accomplish anything. Those holding a different position are now vilified and hated. Each side views the other side as more than just wrong, but evil.

Rather than a peaceful transition of power, the opposition party (Democrats) rejected the latest Republican President and sought to have him removed from office. In their attempt to void the will of the people who voted for President Trump, they falsely accused him of doing criminal things he never did. When that failed, the Democrats attempted to impeach the President over a mere phone call by reading corrupt motives into the actual words that were spoken. Even if the Democrats were somehow able to know what the President's motives were (which is incredulous), based upon the text of the conversation made available to them, they still would not be able to prove a wrong motive.

Never have the two parties been more divided. This divisiveness is, of course, exactly what the enemies of America want to create. Their efforts to prevent unity have been aided by a media that daily spews false accusations and conspiracy theories about Republicans while avoiding any coverage of the many atrocities committed by Democrats. After extensive research, Sharyl Attkisson, a five-time Emmy Award winner and recipient of the Edward R. Murrow Award, exposed the media malfeasance by reporting over 135 media "mistakes" made by *CNN*, *The New York Times*, *The Washington Post*, *USA Today*, *Newsweek*, *Time*, *ABC*, *CBS*, *NBC*, *MSNBC*, and even the *Associated Press* (*AP*). Many of these inaccurate stories were reported by more than one of these media outlets. All of these fake news accounts were directed at President Trump and other Republicans in a way to paint them in a negative way.

Just the facts

For example:

On January 20, 2017, Zeke Miller of *Time* reported that President Trump had removed the bust statue of civil rights leader Martin Luther King Jr. from the Oval Office. The news went viral. It was false.

On June 4, 2017, NBC News reported in a Tweet that Russian President Vladimir Putin told TV host Megyn Kelly that he had compromising information about Trump. Actually, Putin said the opposite: that he did not have compromising information on Trump.

On June 6, 2017, CNN's Gloria Borger, Eric Lichtblau, Jake Tapper and Brian Rokus; and ABC's Justin Fishel and Jonathan Karl reported that Comey was going to refute Donald Trump's claim that Comey told Trump three times he was not under investigation. Instead, Comey did the opposite and confirmed Trump's claim.

On November. 6, 2017, CNN edited a video that made it appear as though Trump impatiently dumped a box of fish food into the water while feeding fish at Japan's palace. The New York Daily News, the Guardian and others wrote stories implying Trump was gauche and impetuous. The full video showed that Trump had simply followed the lead of Japan's Prime Minister.

On January 15, 2018, AP's Laurie Kellman and Jonathan Drew reported that a new report showed trust in the media had fallen during the Trump presidency. But the report that AP cited was actually over a year old and was conducted while Obama was president.

On May 28, 2018, The New York Times' Magazine editor-in-chief Jake Silverstein and CNN's Hadas Gold shared a story with photos of immigrant children in cages as if they were new photos taken under the Trump administration. The article and photos were actually from 2014 under the Obama administration.

On October 13, 2019, ABC aired a video purportedly showing a "slaughter" and "horrific report of atrocities" against Kurds by Turkey after President Trump withdrew U.S. troops. The video was not a combat video at all. It was a file tape of a training show in the U.S.

On November 28, 2019, Newsweek falsely reported that President Trump was spending Thanksgiving golfing in Florida at his Mar-a-Lago Resort. He was actually in Afghanistan serving dinner to U.S. troops. It was the second year in a row that the national media had made the same mistake.

On December 27, 2019, The New York Times published a report to demonstrate how people who voted for Donald Trump no longer support him. Their featured example was a man who – it turns out – never voted for Trump in the first place.

On January 7, 2020, MSNBC wrongly reports up to 30 U.S. deaths after an Iranian rocket attack. In fact, no Americans were killed. The number was a fabricated number reported by the Iranians.

On February 26, 2020, amid the coronavirus outbreak, multiple media outlets implied or stated that President Trump had slashed, cut or gutted the budget for the Centers for Disease Control. In fact, the CDC budget has increased each year.

On March 30, 2020, CBS This Morning airs a story supposedly showing video of a New York hospital crowded with coronavirus patients. Some viewers recognized it as the same video shown to represent a hospital in Italy. CBS News issues a correction saying the network mistakenly used the Italy video in the U.S. story: "It was an editing mistake."

A week later (April 8, 2020), CBS News uses the same Italy video to demonstrate how hospitals in Pennsylvania are overrun with coronavirus cases.

On April 22, 2020, several news outlets claimed President Trump tapped a "former Labradoodle breeder... to lead the U.S. pandemic task force." They implied that the official, Brian Harrison, was unqualified and blamed him for supposed slowing of the U.S. coronavirus response. However, Harrison never led the coronavirus task force. Additionally, while he did briefly own a family business raising Labradoodles, he had also served three administrations in high level posts and was not plucked from dog breeding obscurity to serve on the pandemic task force.

Over one hundred additional examples could be sited. In most of these cases, even after the reports were publicly exposed as falsehoods, there were seldom any retractions or apologies made for the slanderous accusations. The complete list of lies and inaccuracies can be found at Attkisson's blog, "Media Mistakes in the Trump Era," posted June 23, 2020.[28]

Attkisson points out that these many false reports cannot be dismissed as simply sloppy reporting. For one, the reporters are professionals who, in most cases, have had years of experience in journalism. Secondly, there have never been this many fraudulent stories produced by the main stream media in such a short period of time in reporting history. Finally, all the "mistakes" were made in one direction, against Republicans. It is obvious, therefore, that there was bias and even maleficence involved.

One particularly repugnant way Democrats and the mainstream media have attempted to keep America from being one nation under God is to demonize Republicans by portraying them as racists. By labeling all Republicans as racists, the Democrats can justify their unwillingness to work with Republicans. After all, you can't blame someone for not wanting to cooperate with people who are evil.

This false portrayal of Republicans is particularly ironic given the history of the Democratic party. Members of the Democratic Party have always espoused racism more than

Republicans. The KKK itself was founded by ex-confederate soldiers who, after the civil war, supported the Democrat Party.

History of the Ku Klux Klan

Columbia University historian, Eric Foner observed, "In effect, the Klan was a military force serving the interests of the Democratic Party, the planter class, and all those who desired restoration of white supremacy. Its purposes were to destroy the Republican Party's infrastructure, undermine the Reconstruction state, reestablish control of the black labor force, and restore racial subordination in every aspect of Southern life."[29] In his book "White Terror," University of North Carolina historian, Allen Trelease, described the Klan as the "terrorist arm of the Democratic Party."

Founded in 1865, the Ku Klux Klan (KKK) extended into almost every southern state by 1870 and became a vehicle for white southern resistance to the Republican Party's Reconstruction-era policies aimed at establishing political and economic equality for Black Americans. Its members waged an underground campaign of intimidation and violence directed at white and black Republican leaders. Though Congress passed legislation designed to curb Klan terrorism, the organization saw its primary goal–the reestablishment of white supremacy–fulfilled through Democratic victories in state legislatures across the South in the 1870s.[30]

Klan violence worked to suppress black voting, and campaign seasons were deadly. More than 2,000 people were killed, wounded, or otherwise injured in Louisiana within a few weeks prior to the Presidential election of November 1868. Although St Landry Parish had a registered Republican majority of 1,071, after the murders, no Republicans voted in the fall elections. White Democrats cast the full vote of the parish for President Grant's opponent. The KKK killed and wounded more than 200 black Republicans, hunting and chasing them through the woods. Thirteen captives were taken from jail and shot; a half-buried pile of 25 bodies was found in the woods. The KKK made people vote Democratic and gave them certificates of the fact.[31]

The sheer number of Democrat politicians who were members of the KKK compared to the number of Republicans evidences the fact that it was the Democrats who were the more racist party. Below is a list of the more prominent Democrat politicians who were members of the Ku Klux Klan.

Democrats cannot take the moral high ground on racism.

1. Senator Robert C. Byrd was a recruiter for the Klan, rising to the title of Kleagle and Exalted Cyclops of his local chapter. He eventually became the Democratic Party leader in the Senate.

2. Senator Hugo Black was a justice of the Supreme Court of the United States who claimed the only reason he joined the KKK was to get Democratic votes for his Senatorial bid.
3. Theodore G. Bilbo was Governor of Mississippi and U.S. Senator for Mississippi who stated publicly that he was a member of the KKK.
4. John Brown Gordon was a U.S. Senator and was a founder of the KKK in his home state of Georgia.
5. Joseph E. Brown was also a U.S. Senator from Georgia and was a key supporter of the KKK.
6. Elmer David Davies was a Federal Judge of the United States for the Middle District of Tennessee and was a member of the KKK.
7. David Bibb Graves, with the secret endorsement of the Ku Klux Klan, was elected Governor of Alabama. Graves was almost certainly the Exalted Cyclops (chapter president) of the Montgomery chapter of the Klan.
8. Clifford Mitchel Walker, Governor of Georgia, was revealed to be a Klan member by the press in 1924.
9. George Gordon, Congressman for Tennessee's 10th congressional district, was one of the Klan's first members. In 1867, Gordon became the Klan's first Grand Dragon for the Realm of Tennessee, and wrote its *Precept*, a book describing its organization, purpose, and principles.
10.John Tyler Morgan was a U.S. Senator for Alabama and was the Grand Dragon of the KKK

in Alabama.

11. Edmund Pettus was also a U.S. Senator for Alabama and was also a Grand Dragon of the KKK in Alabama.

12. John W. Morton was the Tennessee Secretary of State and was the founder of the Nashville chapter of the KKK.

13. William L. Saunders was the North Carolina Secretary of State and was the founder of the North Carolina chapter.

14. John Clinton Porter was a member of the Klan in the early 1920s and served as mayor of Los Angeles.

15. Benjamin F. Stapleton was mayor of Denver in the 1920s–1940s. He was a Klan member in the early 1920s and appointed fellow Klansmen to positions in municipal government.

16. David Duke was a politician who ran in both Democrat and Republican presidential primaries and was openly involved in the leadership of the Ku Klux Klan. He was founder and Grand Wizard of the Knights of the Ku Klux Klan in the mid-1970s and ran for president in the 1988 Democratic presidential primaries. In 1989 Duke switched political parties.

Unlike the Democrats who elected Robert Byrd and made him party leader in the Senate right up until his death in 2010, the Republican Party has not elected a former member of the KKK in almost 100 years. You have to go back to 1925, to find any

Republican politicians who were members of the KKK, and they were not congressmen.

One was Edward L. Jackson who became Governor of Indiana in 1925. Jackson's administration came under fire for granting undue favor to the Klan's agenda and associates. Jackson ended his political career in disgrace.

The other was Clarence Morley who was Governor of Colorado from 1925 to 1927. He was a KKK member and attempted to have the University of Colorado fire all Jewish and Catholic professors. He only served one two-year term.[32]

Who are the real racists?

In addition to having far more Klansman than the Republicans, from 1800 through 1861 there were seven Democratic presidents who owned slaves.

From 1840 through 1860, there were six Democratic Party convention platforms supporting slavery.

Democrats created the "Jim Crow laws." Jim Crow laws were state and local laws that enforced racial segregation in the Southern United States. These laws were enacted in the late 19th and early 20th centuries by white Democratic dominated state legislatures to disenfranchise and remove political and economic gains made by Black people during the Reconstruction period. Jim Crow laws and Jim Crow state constitutional provisions mandated the segregation of public schools, public places, and public transportation, and the segregation of restrooms, restaurants, and drinking fountains between white and Black people. The Jim Crow laws were enforced until 1965.

The 1857 *Dred Scott* decision was made by Democratic pro-slavery Supreme Court justices. The Court ruled (7–2) that a slave (Dred Scott) who had resided in a free state and territory (where slavery was prohibited) was not entitled to his freedom, and that African Americans were not and could never be citizens of the United States.

Democrats opposed the 13th, 14th, and 15th Amendments to the Constitution. The 13th banned slavery. The 14th granted citizenship and equal protection under the law to anyone born in the United States. It effectively overturned the infamous 1857 *Dred Scott* decision. The 15th gave black Americans the right to vote.

Democrats opposed the Civil Rights Act of 1866, the Civil Rights Act of 1870, the Civil Rights Acts of 1871, and the Civil Rights Act of 1875.

Democrats segregated the federal government, at the direction of Democrat President Woodrow Wilson upon taking office in 1913.

The Democratic Convention of 1924, which was held in Madison Square Garden, consisted of hundreds of delegates who were members of the Ku Klux Klan. As a result, the plank condemning Klan violence was defeated outright. To celebrate, the Klan staged a rally with 10,000 hooded Klansmen in a field in New Jersey directly across the Hudson from the site of the convention. Attended by hundreds of cheering Democratic National

Convention delegates, the rally featured burning crosses and calls for violence against African Americans and Catholics.

Even into the 1960's, Democrats like Alabama Governor George Wallace and Birmingham, Alabama Public Safety Commissioner, Bull Connor, fought against civil rights, unleashing dogs and turning fire hoses on civil rights protestors. Bull Connor was in fact – yes indeed – a member of both the Democratic National Committee and the Ku Klux Klan.

In 1964, on the floor of the U.S. Senate, Democrats held the longest filibuster in American history (54 days) in an attempt to prevent the passing of one thing: The Civil Rights Act.

Three-fourths of the opposition to the 1964 Civil Rights Bill in the U.S. House came from Democrats and 80% of the "nay" vote in the Senate came from Democrats.

Martin Luther King fought against racism while Democratic President John F. Kennedy and Attorney General Robert Kennedy wiretapped both King and his organizer, A. Phillip Randolph. On April 4, 1968, King was assassinated by James Earl Ray, a Democrat.

Contrast all these facts with what Republicans have done to improve the lives of Black Americans.

Republicans are not racists.

The Republican Party was formed in 1854 as an anti-slavery party with Abraham Lincoln as their first president. It was Republicans who fought a bloody civil war to end slavery. It was members of the Republican Party that elected a President who wrote the Emancipation Proclamation to end slavery. Democrats were furious at Lincoln and resisted Black America gaining political power. It was a Democrat, John Wilkes Booth, who assassinated Lincoln in 1865.

Despite Democratic opposition, the Civil Rights Act of 1866 was passed by a Republican Congress. The law was designed to provide blacks with the right to own private property, sign contracts, sue and serve as witnesses in a legal proceeding.

It was Republicans who ratified the 13th, 14th, and 15th Amendments to the Constitution.

It was Republicans who passed the enforcement acts, also known as the Ku Klux Klan acts, designed to enforce the Fourteenth and Fifteenth Amendments as well as the Civil Rights Act of 1866.

The Enforcement Act of 1870 prohibited discrimination by state officials in voter registration on the basis of race, color, or previous condition of servitude. It established penalties for interfering with a person's right to vote and gave federal courts the power to enforce the act. The act banned the use of terror, force or bribery to prevent people from voting because of their race.

There were other Enforcement Acts passed in 1871 by Republicans over Democrat resistance. The first one placed administration of national elections under the control of the federal government and empowered federal judges and United States marshals to supervise local polling places. The Force Act, dated April, 1871, empowered the president to use the armed forces to combat those who conspired to deny equal protection of the laws.

It was Republican Congressmen who passed the Civil Rights Act of 1875, despite Democrats' opposition. It was signed into law by Republican President Ulysses S. Grant. The law prohibited racial discrimination in public places and public accommodations.

While four Democratic platforms from 1908 to 1920 were silent on blacks, segregation, lynching and voting rights as racial problems in the country mounted, the GOP platforms of those years specifically addressed the "Rights of the Negro" (1908) and opposition to lynching (in 1912, 1920, 1924, 1928).

A greater percentage of Republicans (78%) voted for the 1964 Civil Rights Bill than did Democrats. It was Democrats who strongly opposed the bill. It was Democrat Senator, Robert C. Byrd, who filibustered against the bill in an attempt to prevent its passage. The bill outlawed discrimination based on race, color, religion, sex, or national origin. It prohibited unequal application of voter registration requirements, and racial segregation in schools, employment, and public accommodations.

The difference continues to be true.

Even today, Republicans better serve the needs of America's black citizenry. In just the last three years, Republicans have done more for African Americans than the Democrats have done in the last decade. A Republican President (Trump) accomplished acts to assist black Americans that a Democrat President (Obama) promised but never delivered.

In 2017, soon after being elected, President Trump appointed an African American, Dr. Ben Carson, as the United States Secretary of Housing and Urban Development. Under Dr. Carson's leadership over 8,700 Opportunity Zones have been established in low income communities across the country. Opportunity zones are designed to spur economic development and job creation by bringing private investment to areas that might otherwise have difficulty attracting it.

As a result of Trump's policies, African American unemployment reached an all-time low.

President Trump has appropriated more money than any other president to Historically Black Colleges and Universities (HBCU). The President signed legislation to increase federal funding for HBCUs by 13%, the highest level ever. In addition, Trump signed the Future Act into law. The law permanently funds HBCUs and simplifies the FAFSA application.

As a result of the First Step Act, more than 3,000 Americans have been released from prison, and 90% of those who have had their sentences reduced are black Americans. The First Step Act shortens mandatory minimum sentences for nonviolent drug crimes and provides judges greater liberty to go around mandatory minimums. While Obama talked about doing something about prison reform, Trump actually accomplished it.

Despite his many accomplishments, Democrats successfully convince people that he and all Republicans are racists. In doing so, they divide the country along racial lines rather than working with Republicans to unite the country. All this division works to further the radical leftists' aim of destroying America. Democrats publicly support hate groups like Antifa who riot in the streets, burn down buildings, set fire to police cars, tear up public property, and destroy minority owned businesses. Whether deliberately or ignorantly, Democrats are helping to further the neo-Marxists' goal of establishing socialism in America.

CHAPTER 5: SILENCING FREE SPEECH

Frederick Douglass once said, "Liberty is meaningless where the right to utter one's thoughts and opinions has ceased to exist."

George Orwell said, "If liberty means anything at all, it means the right to tell people what they do not want to hear."

John Milton said, "Give me the liberty to know, to utter, and to argue freely according to conscience, above all liberties."

Associate Justice Louis Brandeis stated, "If there be time to expose through discussion the falsehood and fallacies, to avert the evil by the processes of education, the remedy to be applied is more speech, not enforced silence."

All these highly intelligent men understood the importance of free speech in maintaining a just society. Our nation's founding fathers also recognized the critical role free speech plays in insuring the continuation of democracy. The very first Amendment to the constitution grants all Americans the right to free speech. Many state constitutions do as well.

The United States is not alone in this understanding. Freedom of expression is recognized as a human right under article 19 of the Universal Declaration of Human Rights (UDHR) and recognized in international human rights law in the International Covenant on Civil and Political Rights (ICCPR). Article 19 of the UDHR states that "everyone shall have the right to hold opinions without interference," and "everyone shall have the right to freedom of expression; this right shall include freedom to seek, receive and impart information and ideas of all kinds, regardless of frontiers, either orally, in writing or in print, in the form of art, or through any other media of his choice".

James Fee stated, "Freedom of speech is a principle that supports the freedom of an individual or a community to articulate their opinions and ideas without fear of retaliation, censorship, or legal sanction.[33]

Freedom of speech is fiercely protected by America's courts. In 1977, the Supreme Court ruled that even Nazis had the right to free speech and to march in Skokie, Illinois, despite the chilling effect their march was likely to have on the Holocaust survivors who lived in the area.[34]

What is noteworthy about that Supreme Court ruling is that it allowed free speech even though it would obviously offend people. In fact, the very intention of the Nazis was to offend the Jews. The route of the march was deliberately designed to pass by the homes of a Jewish community.

Thus, those who think that offensive speech should be banned are attempting to destroy America's longstanding jurisprudence. Laws against offensive speech are subjective and easily abused. Banning speech because someone finds it offensive gives everyone an incentive to take offence—a fact that opportunistic politicians with ethnic-based support are quick to exploit.

The constitution does not grant anyone the right not to be offended. Yet, that supposed "right" is being used to prevent people from exercising their constitutional right to free speech. If you doubt this is happening, consider just a half dozen situations that have occurred in America in the past few years to censure free speech.

1. The banning of teachers from reading the Bible to students in class or of mentioning anything about intelligent design.

2. The IRS scandal under the Obama administration. The IRS delayed or denied approval of non-profit conservative groups for obviously political reasons. Lois Lerner, head of the IRS, basically admitted as much.

3. The screening of conservative voices from social media platforms.

For example, various studies have found that Facebook and Google, among other social media platforms, engage in censorship against conservatives. Researchers from *The Western Journal,* for example, discovered that conservative publishers have lost an average of nearly 14 percent of their traffic from Facebook, while liberal publishers have gained about 2 percent more web traffic from Facebook than they were getting prior to the algorithm changes implemented in early February.

Facebook has banned several conservatives, labeling them "dangerous," even though they did nothing to violate any of the site's terms. At the same time, Facebook continues to allow left-wing hate speech, including terrorist groups such as Hamas and Hezbollah. Another left-wing group, Redneck Revolt, has distributed training manuals that include sections on "kidnapping," "executions," "sabotage," and "terrorism," yet, they still operate freely on Facebook. Apparently, Mark Zuckerberg considers these hate groups less dangerous than conservatives.

Two African American women going by the names Diamond and Silk regularly posted messages on Facebook which were pro-Trump. Their views were deemed "unsafe to the community." Facebook CEO Mark Zuckerberg assured lawmakers during his congressional testimony that the "unsafe to the community" label was a technical error.

4. The firing of media columnists because they commit the unpardonable sin of being politically incorrect by supporting a conservative position or individual – even once. A few examples include:

- Kevin Williamson from The Atlantic expressed his opinion that abortion is murder. He was fired.
- Republican Congressman Tom Cotton submitted an article to the *The New York*

Times in which he supported use of the military to keep the peace in American cities. The op-ed director of the *Times* accepted it. He was fired.

- Bari Weiss, a (relatively) moderate editor for the NYT was the victim of intense harassment from fellow journalists who disliked some of her views. Some of them were too conservative. After three years of these vicious attacks, she couldn't take it anymore. She resigned. She claimed it was a hostile and threatening work environment. In her resignation letter she stated that "a new consensus has emerged in the press, but perhaps especially at this paper: that truth isn't a process of collective discovery, but an orthodoxy already known to an enlightened few whose job is to inform everyone else."

- Attempts by liberals to get conservative TV personalities fired are rampant. Their tactics include lawsuits, boycotts, and bullying of advertisers who appear on a conservative's program. Liberal Media Matters circulated a list of advertisers for the Fox TV network, encouraging liberals to put pressure on the companies that were involved. "Ingraham Angle" advertisers especially were fiercely attacked. Fox News stood by Ingraham but at the cost of over a dozen advertisers boycotting her show.

5. Even non-media citizens are fired from their jobs because they expressed a conservative viewpoint.

For example, during the heated debate in California over Proposition 8 on the prohibition of same-sex marriage, disclosure laws were used to identify supporters of the proposition. They not only found their names readily available online, but opponents of the measure created a searchable map that identified the homes and addresses of supporters. Many found themselves subject to flash-mob protesters and other forms of harassment. Some of those identified lost their jobs. One of those was Mozilla CEO and Javascript inventor, Brendan Eich. He was forced to resign for his thought crime: supporting marriage as the union of a man and a woman, and not recanting.

Google engineer James Damore was fired for drafting a memo that questioned his company's policies regarding gender.

The Women's National Basketball Association has been asked to take ownership away from the Atlanta Dream team owner, Karen Loeffler, simply because she disagreed with the goals of the Black Lives Matters Movement. She is a Republican Senator running for re-election.

It should come as no surprise to learn that a recent Cato Institute survey found that nearly a third of Americans fear their political opinions could cost them their job. Their fears are well founded. The survey also found that half of those who self-identified as "strong liberals" support the firing of an executive who personally donated to President

Trump. As a result, those who self-identified as Republican had the highest percentage (77%) of those stating that they practiced self-censorship. Only those who self-identified as "strong liberals" had a majority who stated they were *not* afraid to tell others their political beliefs. Perhaps, the reason they are unafraid to freely express themselves is because few try to take away their freedom of speech.

6. Protesting and disrupting invited conservative speakers on college and university campuses.

For example, students at Columbia University booed and shouted down all the speakers from the Minutemen organization when they came to speak on campus. The students interrupted Mr. Stewart, who is African-American, when he referred to the Declaration of Independence's self-evident truth that "All men are created equal," calling him a racist, a sellout, and a black white supremacist. When Jim Gilchrist, founder of the Minutemen, was introduced student protestors stormed the stage attacking Gilchrist. Gilchrist had to be escorted off stage for his safety.[35]

This kind of situation is happening on campuses all across the country. Students no longer believe that Americans have the right to free speech. Forty-four percent of surveyed students told the Brookings Institution that they do *not* believe that the First Amendment protects free speech, compared with the 39 percent who believe that it does. A full 20 percent of respondents maintained it acceptable to inflict physical harm on those deemed to have made "offensive and hurtful statements."

The motto of previous generations was, "I disapprove of what you say, but I will defend to the death your right to say it." The motto of today's students is, "Your rights depend on my feelings, and if my feelings are hurt, then you must shut up."

How does it end?

All these aforementioned efforts to silence free speech inevitably lead to a dangerous end. It ultimately leads to a country that bans the expression of anything not considered acceptable by those in power. The government will control what is allowed to be said, read, or viewed by the citizenry. This is what Hitler did in Germany. This is what socialist countries do. This is why those desiring America to become a socialist nation are working so hard to silence dissenting voices. All those who think free speech should be controlled would be wise to read books like "Animal Farm" or "1984" by George Orwell or "Brave New World" by Alex Huxley.

CHAPTER 6: BANKRUPTING AMERICA

According to the EPA, if the United States reduced its carbon emissions down to zero, it would reduce the overall emissions in the world by less than 15%. Even if it *were* possible to eliminate 100% of the carbon emissions from the U.S., the only major difference it would make would be to totally destroy the economy. Despite this reality, global warming alarmists want America to spend trillions of dollars toward accomplishing that goal. Just switching from fossil fuels to low-carbon sources of energy such as solar and wind power is estimated to cost $44 trillion between now and 2050, according to a report released by the International Energy Agency. America's debt load is already over 23 trillion dollars and increasing exponentially. Many economists think that our present debt situation alone will eventually lead us into economic collapse. According to the 2020 annual report of the Social Security Board of Trustees, the trust funds that disburse retirement, disability and other Social Security benefits will be depleted by 2035. Add that to the economic downturn due to the covid-19 pandemic, and you have the makings of a complete financial meltdown.

All these facts do not deter the global warming alarmists. That's because many actually desire to see America bankrupted, because that will end the country's capitalistic system and make way for their socialistic one. Thus, their major concern is not climate change but the destruction of a country they view as evil. Ultimately, these neo-Marxists wish to take over both the economy and the country itself. It comes down to power and control. Evidence that their concern for environmental protection is just a ruse can be found in the fact that whole idea that the earth is doomed to destruction due to global warming is merely a theory and not a provable fact.

Does global warming mean the earth is doomed to destruction?

When I was in high school, every student received a weekly newspaper appropriately named the *Weekly Reader*. I remember some of the articles declaring that scientists were predicting another ice age would be coming to the earth in the near future. I don't remember all the data they used to justify their prediction. It may have been that, at the time, the earth's temperature readings had gone down for more than one year in a row. It may have been based on the sun's reduction in size over time. Whatever the data was, the scientists were convinced the polar ice caps were going to continue to grow until the entire earth would be covered with ice. Anyone who dared question their findings were considered to be anti-science.

Now just the opposite is being predicted. Today's scientists claim the earth will soon become so warm that the polar ice caps will melt and flood the earth. Once again, all doubters of their prediction are considered to be anti-science. This recent prediction is based primarily on the fact that the earth's temperature has been increasing slightly for more than one year in a row. While this is true, some scientists believe that the earth's temperature has always fluctuated up and down. Sometimes it will go up annually for a few years and then go down for a number of years. If we reject these particular scientists' theory, are we to be considered anti-science?

97% of all scientists believe.

Alarmists continually state that 97% of the world's scientists believe man has caused global warming. It has been stated so often that almost everyone believes it to be true, even though it is not. Few even know where that statistic came from. The 97 percent figure derives from two severely flawed surveys. One survey involved 10,257 people with a self-interest in human-induced global warming, who published "science" supported by taxpayer-funded research grants. In other words, they were scientists who were expected to come up with the findings they did. "Scientific researchers know that public funding, scientific awards, and academic promotions go to the environmentally correct."[36] This statement was made by Judith Curry, a climatologist who once headed the department of earth and atmospheric sciences at the Georgia Institute of Technology. She gave up on the academy so that she could express herself independently because, she said, "Independence of mind and climatology have become incompatible."

Not only did the survey involve highly paid researchers, but replies from 3146 respondents were whittled down to 77 self-appointed climate "scientists" of whom 75 were judged to agree that human-induced warming was taking place. Thus, the 97 percent figure was derived from a group with only 75 members. What were the criteria for rejecting the 3069 respondents? There was no mention in the study of why, or that 75 out of 3146 is only 2.38 percent. While only 2.38 percent of the climate scientists agreed that humans have played a significant role in changing climate, the study reported that the percentage was 97.

Another "study" claimed that published scientific papers showed there was a 97.1 percent consensus that man had caused at least half of the global warming since 1950. How was this 97.1% figure determined? By "inspection" of 11,944 published papers. This "inspection," however, was nothing close to being rigorous scholarship.

The study was actually a compilation of opinions from non-scientific, politically motivated volunteer activists who used a search engine for key words in 11,944 scientific papers. They did not consider, if they even understood, the scientific context of the use of "global warming" and "global climate change." Nor did they read the complete papers, and so were unable to critically evaluate the diversity of the science published therein.

After the original 11,944 papers were read by real scientists, they came to the diametrically opposite conclusion. Of the 11,944 papers, only 41 explicitly stated that humans caused most of the warming since 1950 (0.3 percent). Of the 11,944 climate "science" papers, less than 2 percent said that carbon dioxide caused most of the global warming since 1950. Not one paper endorsed a man-made global warming catastrophe.[37]

John Cook, who runs the popular website "SkepticalScience.com," was one of the key authors of the study. According to him, he found that over 97 percent [of papers he surveyed] endorsed the view that the Earth is warming up and human emissions of greenhouse gases are the main cause. However, Cook misrepresented the findings of over 98% of the papers he used in the study. As a result, numerous scientists whose papers were classified by Cook publicly protested.

Dr. Richard Tol said, "Cook's survey included 10 of my 122 eligible papers. 5/10 were rated incorrectly. 4/5 were rated as endorse rather than neutral."

Dr. Craig Idso declared, "That is not an accurate representation of my paper . . ."

Dr. Nir Shaviv, also said, "It is not an accurate representation."

Dr. Nicola Scafetta claimed that, "Cook et al. (2013) is based on a strawman argument . . ."

Falsifying the evidence

Climate change advocates might argue that scientists do not deliberately falsify their research. Really? Such advocates are obviously unaware of the mountain of hacked emails that show that scientists who held the public trust regarding information on climate change research had been dishonest about it. The personal emails and documents were taken from the University of East Anglia's (UEA) servers in November of 2009 and leaked on to the internet.

There was evidence that a series of measurements from Chinese weather stations were seriously flawed, and that documents relating to them could not be produced. A great deal of information was withheld, despite multiple requests under freedom of information laws. Of the 105 freedom of information requests to the university concerning the climatic research unit (CRU), up to the end of December, only 10 had been released in full.

Two years later, in 2011, another batch of 5,000 emails were released to the public. The emails were among scientists central to the assertion that humans are causing a global warming crisis. Three things were discovered from the released emails: (1) prominent scientists central to the global warming debate were taking measures to conceal rather than disseminate underlying data and discussions; (2) these scientists viewed global warming as a political "cause" rather than a balanced scientific inquiry, and (3) many of these scientists frankly admit to each other that much of the science is weak and dependent on deliberate manipulation of facts and data.

The emails show scientists selectively expunged data and suppressed research not supporting the conclusions they wanted. Any facts that did not support man-made global warming were ignored and remain unreported. If this sounds eerily familiar, it should. Scientists have done the same thing to support their theory of macroevolution (see chapter 6).

As with macro-evolution, the theory of earth's destruction by global warming is just that – a theory. Based on this theory, it is now being predicted that the earth will be destroyed in less than twenty-five years. Nobody is certain of a weather prediction that tells us what is going to happen 24 hours in advance. Now we're asked to believe a prediction of what is going to happen 24 years into the future? If a 24-hour prediction of weather is wrong almost as often as it is right, why would anyone think that a 24-year prediction is a certainty? As the Danish physicist Niels Bohr said, "Prediction is very difficult, especially if it is about the future." So far, predictions by advocates of the theory have been consistently wrong.

On December 13 & 14, 2009, Al Gore referenced "state-of-the-art" computer modeling when he stated the following: "Some of the models suggest that there is a 75 percent chance that the entire north polar ice cap, during some of the summer months, could be completely ice-free within the next five to seven years." Gore made this statement at COP15 Copenhagen which ran from Dec 7 – Dec 18, 2009. Thus, the prediction was to occur by the year 2014. What has really happened since then?

Largely unreported data

According to official government data from the National Snow & Ice Data Center (NSIDC), Arctic Sea Ice is once again growing, with current 2020 levels exceeding 8 out of the previous 10 years. NSIDC uses NASA satellites to collect data.[38]

The Danish Meteorological Institute (DMI) states that we have clear evidence that the ice at the poles is now not only *not melting*, it is in fact once again *growing*, in both thickness and extent. This growth is especially obvious in Antarctica.[39]

The satellites used by the Gravity Recovery and Climate Experiment (GRACE) show that there is even a small increase in the mass of the ice on Greenland. GRACE is a partnership between NASA and the German Research Centre for Geosciences (GFZ).[40]

While Mount Kilimanjaro's glacier is still shrinking, some scientists believe the shrinkage is due more to deforestation than to global warming. **One study done** by Nicholas Pepin, a lecturer in climatology and meteorology at Portsmouth, found that the shrinking Furtwängler Glacier—once an enormous icecap that sat atop Kilimanjaro's summit—is strongly related to tree removal.[41] **More recently, it was discovered that the reason** some ice glaciers are melting faster is due to volcano activity occurring underneath the glaciers. Research by the National Science Foundation has reported this to be true. An international team of scientists from NSF and the U.K.'s Natural Environmental Research Council discovered an underwater heat source by tracing the chemical signature of helium indicating underwater volcanic activity.[42] West Antarctica alone is thought to contain well over 100 volcanoes.

Are all these scientific facts to be ignored? Apparently, they are. There is real truth in the saying, "It's easier to fool people than to convince them that they have been fooled."[43]

The late writer/physician Michael Crichton pointed out, in a speech he gave at the California Institute of Technology, that common sense was being violated in the research allegedly showing that human activity is causing the earth's climate to irreversibly warm.

Albert Einstein advised that the safest bet is to be your own fact-checker (as best you can), as "blind belief in authority is the greatest enemy of the truth."

For hundreds of years, astronomers have been counting sunspots. Cycles of sunspot activity correspond with records of climate change. Results from the study of sunspots have led some scientists to expect global cooling in about 30 years.

This theory is based on the number of sunspots and *galactic cosmic rays* (GCRs) which enter the earth's atmosphere. GCRs are mainly proton particles. When these fast-moving protons collide with molecules in our atmosphere, a shower of charged particles, or *ions*, is produced. Many scientists suspect these charged particles influence cloud behavior, which affects global weather and climate. The number of cosmic rays entering the atmosphere can vary 15% over the course of a solar cycle, which is every eleven years. There are two main schools of thought on how GCRs could affect weather and climate. One model was designed by Danish physicist Dr. Henrik Svensmark and the other model by Dr. Brian Tinsley, professor emeritus of the University of Texas at Dallas. If either of these two models is correct, then the amount of the earth's carbon emissions is irrelevant when it comes to change in the earth's temperature. Furthermore, based on this theory the earth is more likely to see global cooling rather than global warming in 30 years.

For more details on this theory, see "Cosmic Rays, Sunspots, and Climate Change, Part 1" at https://www.icr.org/article/11802 and Part 2 at https://www.icr.org/article/11854.

Curry, obviously not a member of the "97 Percenters," points out that between 1910 and 1940, the planet warmed during a climatic episode that resembles our own, down to the degree. The warming can't be blamed on industry, she argues, because back then, most of the carbon-dioxide emissions from burning fossil fuels were small. In fact, Curry says, "almost half of the warming observed in the twentieth century came about in the first half of the century, before carbon-dioxide emissions became large. Natural factors thus had to be the cause. None of the climate models used by scientists now working for the United Nations can explain this older trend. Nor can these models explain why the climate suddenly cooled between 1950 and 1970, giving rise to widespread warnings about the onset of a new ice age. I recall magazine covers of the late 1960s or early 1970s depicting the planet in the grip of an annihilating deep freeze. According to a group of scientists, we faced an apocalyptic environmental scenario—but the opposite of the current one."

Curry also stated that, "The sea level is rising, but this has been gradually happening since the 1860s; we don't yet observe any significant acceleration of this process in our time."[44]

Climatologist Pat Michaels put things in perspective by saying, "It's warmed up around 1 degree Celsius since 1900, and life expectancy doubled in the industrialized democracies! Yet, we are to believe that if the temperature ticks up another half a degree, then the entire system crashes. That's the most absurd belief!"

Michaels and Curry are not the only scientists who are not part of the "97 Percenters." Peter Thorne of the UK Met Office wrote, "Observations do not show rising temperatures throughout the tropical troposphere unless you accept one single study and approach and discount a wealth of others." "I also think the science is being manipulated to put a political spin on it which for all our sakes might not be too clever in the long run," Thorne added.[45]

The evidence for immense political pressures being exerted into the science is so great that it cannot be contained in a book this size. Even a separate chapter would not do justice to it as it can be found everywhere. In the interest of brevity, I'll mention just one example which involves the United Nations.

Rajendra Pachauri, an Indian railway engineer who remade himself into a climatologist and became director of the IPCC, admitted that at the UN, he recruited only climatologists convinced of the carbon-dioxide warming explanation, excluding all others. He actually had the hutzpah to admit that the UN was totally biased.[46]

To be clear, I am not suggesting that all scientists are dishonest who believe that the world will soon be destroyed by global warming. Nor am I claiming to know that it won't. What I am saying is that this idea is only a theory. It is not a fact. All of those (including those pushing the "Green New Deal") who state otherwise have either been duped themselves or are deliberately lying, just like those who claim that 97% of scientists believe it.

Do scientists have ulterior motives for their claims?

It might be worth noting that there is greater motivation for believers to lie than there is for nonbelievers. What happens to believers if they turn out to be wrong? They will have to clean up a large amount of egg off their faces. Nonbelievers, on the other hand, know that if they turn out to be wrong, people may die, including themselves. Yet they are so certain of their position, they do not fear such a doomsday. They certainly aren't going to deliberately lie, given the gravity of the consequences if they are mistaken. Additionally, they currently face a great deal of criticism from the majority of people that believers do not. In some cases, nonbelievers are even violently attacked. Believers are motivated by receiving research grants, the applause of the preponderance of others, and prestigious academic awards. Nonbelievers not only lack these incentives, but they are actually faced with disincentives. So, it is fair to ask, "Who is more likely to falsify data?

It must be admitted that scientists who do believe the theory have been far more successful in propagating their view, so much so that the general public now views nonbelievers as being anti-science. This view, however, is based on ignorance, dishonest reporting, and brainwashing.

People today know very little, if any, of the scientific findings that refute the "facts" given by climate change alarmists. As a result, they are convinced the world will soon be destroyed by global warming. No wonder there is so much anxiety today among Americans. The stress caused by this and the COVID-19 pandemic is so high that the number of suicides is now at an all-time high, college students need "safe spaces" on their university campuses in order to lower their anxiety, and many individuals cannot cope without an "emotional support" animal. Most of this fear is based on a theory that has as much scientific evidence against it as it has for it. If the lives lost to suicide are the result of fear due to the catastrophic predictions of global warming, then those deaths become unnecessary tragedies if the theory proves to be false.

Additionally, if America is toppled as a result of bankruptcy due to spending on this cause, and the dire predictions made prove false, then the socialists will have successfully destroyed capitalism from within rather than from attacks from without.

An aside

There is one last side comment I would like to mention before ending this chapter. There are those who believe in God and the Bible who point to the rainbow and claim that it is a sign from God that he will keep his promise to never again flood the earth as he did in Noah's time. From that they conclude that global warming will not cause the glaciers to melt and flood the earth. This is certainly not scientific evidence, but it doesn't mean such believers are wrong. Yet they are ridiculed and seen as ignorant fools simply because they believe the Bible. In fact, anyone who believes in God is accused of having an unscientific mind, especially if they are Christians.

The truth is many of the world's greatest scientists were theists (and most of those were Christians) including Copernicus, Kepler, Newton, Pasteur, Paschal, Fleming, Edwards, Boyle, and Galileo. Likewise, today there are a great many scientists who believe in God despite the common notion that all scientists hold to a completely nontheistic naturalistic world view. There are Christian astronomers, physicists, chemists, and even biologists with high IQ's and extensive educational backgrounds. Some of them are making extraordinary new discoveries in their chosen field. One can believe in science and the Bible without any conflict.

CHAPTER 7: REMOVING GOD FROM AMERICA'S CONSCIOUSNESS

In chapter two, it was pointed out that one of the fundamental strategies of the Marxist playbook is to demonize capitalism as the source of all suffering and oppression. A second fundamental strategy of the Marxist playbook is to undermine Christianity. This is done by co-opting it from within, corrupting it. One way to accomplish this it to redefine the Biblical gospel away from individual salvation through repentance of sin and faith in Jesus Christ to a collective salvation that calls for the world to unite to heal the wrongs and to create a "just" society that eliminates poverty and injustice and creates the kingdom of God on earth through collective salvation. This has been termed the "social gospel." It is fast becoming the main theology of churches throughout the world. This is all leading up to a one-world religion, as prophesied in the book of Revelation.

A second way to undermine Christianity is to contend that Christians stand in the way of progress toward a greater society. When atheistic socialists make this claim, they never mention the multitude of significant contributions Christians have made to society. As already mentioned, it was Christians who developed America's educational system, which includes the establishment of colleges like Harvard and Yale. Christians pioneered some of the most important improvements in health, science, social justice, and charity. As was pointed out in the previous chapter, many of the world's greatest scientists were Christians, including Newton, Pasteur, Kepler, Paschal, Fleming, and Edwards.

Wilberforce, along with Buxton, Macaulay, and Clark, all of them Christians, were the top leaders in ending slavery in the British Empire.

Some of the greatest prison reformers were Christians, including John Howard, Elizabeth Fry, and Theodor Fliedner.

Avowed Christian Anthony Ashley Cooper pioneered the establishment of child-labor laws and founded mental health sanitariums.

Harriett Beecher Stowe was the daughter of a preacher, married a preacher, and all of her brothers were preachers. Her book, *Uncle Tom's Cabin*, ignited the minds and imaginations of people in both the North and the South. "So, this is the little lady who made this big war," said Abraham Lincoln upon meeting her for the first time. Her book had a major impact in ending slavery in America.

Florence Nightingale, whose nursing school in London began modern nursing, saw herself as being in the service of God.

The Red Cross, the YMCA, the Salvation Army, and Barnardo's Homes (world's largest orphanage system) were all started by Christians.

Catholic Charities is the largest social services organization in America helping the poor, the elderly, unwed mothers, the homeless, immigrants, and all people in need.

Humanism vs. Christianity

Atheists might point out that you don't have to be a Christian to do good. Secular humanists have also done good things. That is true, but what is their motivation for doing them? The reason secular humanists believe doing good is admirable is due to the ideals they have learned from a society influenced by religious values. How does a humanist know that giving to the poor is something people should do? It is not because one simply senses it to be right. No, it is because they believe in the Golden Rule. Where did the Golden Rule originate? Even secular humanists know it was not first suggested by a secularist, but that it comes from the Bible.

Furthermore, Christians are more willing to give to the less fortunate than are atheistic humanists. A Barna Survey in 2013 on US giving noted that in the area of charity, Christians donated far more money than those who claimed no faith. A survey conducted by BBC also noted higher giving amongst religious believers than atheists in the UK. While humanists take great pride in fighting (e.g., marching, protesting, indoctrinating others) for what they believe are good causes, they aren't as willing to invest their personal resources in the lives of others as are believers in a Higher Power. Secular humanists are extremely interested in changing the policies of government to aid in their causes, because that involves other people's (taxpayers) money, but they are far less charitable with their own money than are Christians. It is always easier to give lip service to a cause than financial sacrifice.

Finally, when people are governed by atheistic humanism alone, it ultimately results in barbarism and/or tyranny. History has shown this to be true in every situation. Consider, for example, the Roman Empire, Russia under Stalin, or China under Mao. Atheism by its very nature leads to godless atrocities, because people are basically selfish. Humanists, of course, believe people are basically good, but the entire history of man disproves that belief. Left to themselves without the guidance of any religious values, humans become less and less restrained in their immoral behavior. A society based on the beliefs of humanism alone does not move in the direction of improved moral behavior. It's just the opposite. Such societies move toward increased immorality. Humanists will never be able to create the utopian society they think they can because of their unrealistic understanding of human nature.

Are humans able to rule themselves?

Without recognition of God, the standards for moral behavior become subjective and ultimately dangerous. If there is no God, then morality must be determined by man. Agreeing on any one set of standards, however, becomes impossible, since everyone will have their own opinion as to what those standards should be. Who is to say which opinion is correct? Nietzsche preached that a group of "supermen" must rise up with the courage to create their own values through their "will to power." Nietzsche rejected the "soft" values of Christianity (brotherly love, turning the other cheek, charity, compassion, etc.); he felt they hindered man's creativity and potential.[47]

Many other atheists agree with Nietzsche concerning moral relativism. British atheist philosopher Bertrand Russell wrote, "Outside human desires there is no moral standard."[48]

Atheist Alfred J. Ayer believed that moral commands did not result from any objective standard above man. Instead, Ayer stated that moral commands merely express one's subjective feelings. When one says that murder is wrong, one is merely saying that he or she feels that murder is wrong.[49]

Atheist Jean-Paul Sartre, a French existentialist, believed that there is no objective meaning to life. Therefore, according to Sartre, man must create his own values.[50]

Atheist Richard Dawkins stated in an interview, "What's to prevent us from saying Hitler wasn't right? I mean, that is a genuinely difficult question."[51]

If there is no God, then who then is qualified to determine what is right and what is wrong? Atheists claim morality can be determined by reason. Great, but who is qualified to determine what is reasonable? Cannibals consider it reasonable to eat people. After all, this practice not only provides them with nourishing food, but it protects them from being harmed by their enemies (You can't be hurt by someone you have eaten).

The Roman philosopher Seneca the Younger wrote, "We drown even children who at birth are weakly and abnormal,"...stressing that "it is not anger but reason" that provides justification for such an act.[52] What our Judeo-Christian based Western culture might view as horrific, Roman society (which was built upon a godless foundation) practiced based on reason.

Suggesting reason alone is sufficient to direct behavior is intellectually dishonest. Human reason will always be guided by presuppositions. These presuppositions will always prevent humans from agreeing on what is moral and what is not. As a result, everyone ends up doing what is right in their own eyes (Judges 17:6; 21:25; Proverbs 21:2). That is not to say everyone who is an atheist is going to end up a murderer. Certainly, there are many nonbelievers who are benevolent and kind. But while atheists point to these upstanding godless citizens as proof of their theory that you can be good without believing in God, they conveniently ignore the cultural foundations that taught those individuals to be good. As columnist Jeff Jacoby observed, "In our culture, even the most passionate atheist cannot help having been influenced by the Judeo-Christian worldview that shaped Western civilization."[53]

The consequences of humanism

There are tragic consequences that result from a society that has no Divine basis for morality. Over time almost every immoral behavior will be tolerated. Such evil acts as bestiality, rape, and pedophilia will be considered acceptable behavior as soon as the majority of "rational thinkers" see nothing wrong with them. There are already atheists who are open to all of these ideas and more.

The atheist philosopher Peter Singer defends the practice of bestiality. He is also known as a defender of killing the aged (if they have dementia), newborns (for almost any reason until they are two years old), and necrophilia (assuming it's consensual).[54] Despite holding these views, the academic establishment rewarded him with a bioethics chair at Princeton University.[55]

British atheist Christopher Hitchens twice refused to condemn bestiality during the William Lane Craig vs Christopher Hitchens debate.[56]

Atheist PZ Myers wrote about bestiality, "So, to answer clueless thick thick-skulled Christian idiot's question, I don't object to bestiality."[57]

Skatje Myers, the daughter of PZ Myers, describes herself as an atheist and moral nihilist. She wrote the following:

> "Sexual relationships between humans and animals come as such a shock to people, but it doesn't to me. There can be very deep, meaningful relationships between humans and their pets.... That said, I remind you that my position isn't based on my own personal

wants. I just don't see any reason to ban it other than the same reason things like homosexuality and sodomy were banned: it's icky. I think it's bad practice to put social taboos into legislature when no actual logical argument can be made against it."[58]

Christian apologist Kyle Butt wrote: "In my debate with Dan Barker, Barker stated that under certain circumstances, rape would be a moral obligation."[59]

Harry Hay (1912 - 2002) was also an advocate of statutory rape. He was an atheist and a vociferous advocate of man/boy love.[60] In 1986, Hay marched in a gay parade wearing a shirt emblazoned with the words "NAMBLA walks with me."[61]

Atheist David Thorstad was a founding member of the North American Man-Boy Love Association (NAMBLA).[62]

The writer Samuel R. Delaney, an atheist and a homosexual,[63] said he was a supporter of NAMBLA.[64]

John Maynard Keynes' male bed partner, Lytton Strachey, wrote that Keynes was an atheist and a sodomite."[65] Keynes and his friends made numerous trips to the resorts surrounding the Mediterranean. At the resorts, little boys were sold by their families to bordellos which catered to homosexuals.[66]

Yes, bestiality, rape, and pedophilia all fall within the "reasoned" morality of many atheists. It is only a matter of time and continual moral decay before what now seems to be unspeakable acts become legal and commonly practiced in America. It is not enough that some reject a belief in God; it is the goal of atheists to convince everyone that God does not exist.

This brings us to the third way Christianity is being undermined in America through the direct promotion of atheism. Marx said religion was the opium of the people. Stalin, Lenin, and Mao were not only atheists, but they tortured and killed those who believed in God, especially Christians. Right now, in America, those who believe in God and refuse to compromise their biblical standards of morality are ridiculed and persecuted. They're labeled haters, intolerant, bigots, divisive, meanspirited, evil, and unloving. How did a country that was founded as a Christian nation become one that despises Christians?

Start by taking God out of the classroom.

In 1963, atheist Madeline Murray O'Hare challenged the policy of mandatory prayers and Bible reading in public schools in her *Murray v. Curlett* lawsuit. Consolidated with *Abington School District v. Schempp*, it was heard by the United States Supreme Court, which ruled that officially sanctioned mandatory Bible-reading in American public schools was unconstitutional. The previous year, the Supreme Court had prohibited officially sponsored prayer in schools in the lawsuit *Engel v.*

Vitale (1962) on similar grounds. As a result, both prayer and Bible reading were eliminated from public schools. Students no longer learned Christian principles from their teachers. Eventually, educators weren't even allowed to even suggest that a God existed. So, what has been the result of these historic changes in the way students are educated?

Is ignorance bliss?

America's judicial system has not changed significantly in the past thirty-five years but the number of its incarcerated has grown exponentially. In 1979, the number of U.S. citizens imprisoned was less than 500,000. Today the number has ballooned to over 2,300,000 while the general population has only increased from 221 million to 317 million. Adjusted for population, imprisonment has quintupled in this country in the last thirty-five years. If the judicial system has remained relatively the same, what accounts for this massive increase in crime? Something monumental had to have taken place during this time period. The graph below shows the number of prisoners in the United States for each decade from 1920 through 2006.

Notice how the numbers are fairly consistent and low until 1980. Why the colossal spike? The timing of the increase can be traced back to the removal of the Judeo-Christian morality which had previously been taught in our public schools. By 1964, prayer and Bible reading had been completely eliminated from public schools. Thus, six-year old children entering first grade at that time would graduate high school without even once hearing the word God mentioned in their classrooms. They would not be allowed to see (to say nothing of learn) the Ten Commandments upon which our legal system is based. Students would not be encouraged to pray – just the opposite – they would be warned not to pray. They would turn 21 in 1979 and become the first generation of adults who grew up in America thinking God was not important enough to discuss publicly. In fact, in school they learned that teachers could be fired for even suggesting God was a worthy topic for student consideration. After learning atheistic evolution, these now former students could assume God did not even exist. At the very least, He had no bearing on how they should live their lives. Morality was now a mere human issue to be worked out by each individual through values clarification.

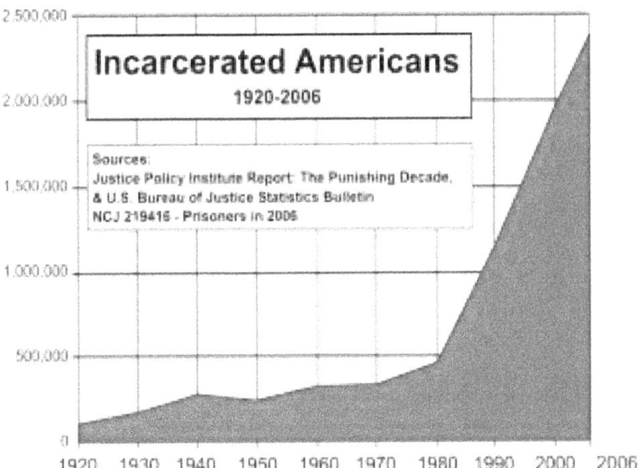

Not surprisingly, fifteen years after this drastic change in curriculum took place (1964) there was an enormous upswing in crime. In 1964, the major problems teachers had to deal with were students running in the halls, talking in class, and chewing gum. Today, teachers deal with students who commit rape, assault, and even murder in their classrooms. Shooting sprees like Columbine were unheard of prior to 1964.

Despite the fact our judicial system continued to work, something had changed to cause citizens to have less and less reluctance to break the law. From 1980 forward, the number of crimes committed each year in America continued to multiply as fewer and fewer people took God seriously.

In addition to the moral decline, America's student academic performances steadily declined as well. During the sixties, students in the United States were ranked number one in the world in academic achievement. By 2003, they weren't even in the top twenty. Today, our students are academically behind such countries as Poland, Latvia, Iceland, New Zealand, Liechtenstein, and the Slovac Republic.

In one international country-by-country comparison of the math, reading, and science skills of 15-year-olds, the United States ranked 28th in the world in mathematics, 18th in the world in reading, and 22nd in the world in science.[67] Removing religious instruction from public schools did not bring intellectual enlightenment. Instead, it brought a rapid decline in moral behavior. Sadly, there is statistical evidence to show that students who entered school after 1964 perform poorer academically and commit more crimes than any previous generation.

Not teaching about God in public school was a major step in the neo-Marxists' efforts to undermine Christianity in America. It was, however, only the beginning. The next step was to zealously teach atheism itself. This plan has also been successfully implemented, as the theory of evolution rather than creationism is now being taught as an alternative explanation for human existence to every student at every grade level. Thus, there is no need for a creator God. The absurdity of this theory will be demonstrated in chapter eight.

In addition, the direct promotion of atheism is persistently interwoven into the curriculum of America's colleges and universities. Many professors openly challenge students to reexamine their "antiquated" beliefs in a supreme being. It is likely this will soon be happening in the country's high schools as well, if it hasn't started to happen already.

Dishonesty in the classroom

A few years ago, my wife took a course in general philosophy from the State University at Albany in upstate New York. Instead of dealing with philosophy in general, however, the professor told the students the entire semester would be dedicated to the discussion of whether or not God exists. It soon became apparent that he was not interested in teaching general philosophy, but in showing the students the absurdity of believing in a supreme being. The final exam was a one-question essay requiring students to state whether they believed in God and tell why or why not. My wife, who is normally an "A" student, wrote why she did, indeed, believe in God. She was not surprised when she received a "D" for her grade.

The professor's basic position was that belief in God is no different from belief in Santa Claus or the tooth fairy. Despite the fact he was intelligent enough to know there are huge differences, he declared they were exactly the same. For example, belief in Santa Claus and the tooth fairy is only shared by children. Belief in God, on the other hand, is held by adults who have the maturity to discern the evidence. Furthermore, after children realize there is no Santa Claus or tooth fairy, they can never again be convinced these fictional characters exist. The amount of evidence for Santa Claus and the tooth fairy is extremely limited (e.g. gifts under the Christmas tree or money under the pillow) and such "evidence" can easily be discredited. The amount of evidence for God, however, is massive and many adults (including atheists) become convinced of His existence after considering the evidence. Chapter 8 will deal with some of the evidence.

God and the Easter bunny

If God does not exist, why waste everyone's time discussing His existence? Imagine if the professor were to spend the entire semester discussing the existence or nonexistence of the Easter bunny. The students would be justifiably outraged and demand their money back. They would feel cheated out of their tuition when they discovered the professor planned to consume their learning opportunity debating the existence of a mythical rabbit. It would be a joke to call such a class a general philosophy course. The professor was unable to see the irony and foolishness of spending an entire semester examining what he considered to be an equivalent to the Easter bunny. If both God and the Easter bunny are only mythical beings then neither topic would be a legitimate discussion for even one day. Such folly is surprising when you consider the professor believed truth is found through reason. Teaching on a subject that doesn't exist is hardly reasonable.

Is God dead?

By teaching atheism, what the professor was doing (whether he knew it or not) was furthering the cause of socialism. Leaders of socialist countries do not want its citizens to believe in or be loyal to anything other than socialism. Belief in God gets in the way of that goal, so either the citizens become atheists or they are exiled, imprisoned, tortured, and even killed. So, have the efforts in America been successful in moving its citizens toward atheism?

The statistics say "yes."

In recent reports, Barna and other researchers have noted that Christianity is on a steady decline while Americans' identification with atheism continues to increase. Barna's tracking data show that in 2003, over eight in 10 Americans identified themselves as Christians. But by 2018, that number had dropped by almost 10 percentage points, from 81 percent to 72 percent. At the same time, Barna found the exact opposite occurred for the number who said they did not believe in God. In 2003, a little over one in 10 Americans (11%) claimed to be atheist, agnostic or of no religion ("none"). Fifteen years later that percentage nearly doubled in size from 11 percent to 21 percent in 2018.

When America was first founded, the vast majority of its citizens identified themselves as Christians and regularly attended church. Today, according to a 2019 survey, only 23 percent of Americans attend church or synagogue every week, compared to 24 percent who seldom attend and another 29 percent of Americans who never attend. Less than a fourth of Americans now see church attendance as an important part of their week. Socialists are, of course, thrilled by these numbers.

CHAPTER 8: ELIMINATING THE NEED FOR A CREATOR

Teaching evolution to every American student accomplishes two things that help socialists advance their cause. Number one, it eliminates the need for a creator God as children learn that God did not breathe life into Adam, but humans evolved from an amoeba. Number two, it devalues human life, opening the door for the acceptance of abortion, euthanasia, and violence that includes the murder of innocent citizens.

Even though the famous "Scopes Monkey Trial" took place in 1925, it was several years later before macroevolution was universally taught as scientific fact. I was a twelve-year old sixth grader when I first read about evolution in a school textbook. Today, the theory is found in science textbooks used by every public school in America, including grade school. The theory is taught as a fact with no disclaimers or questions regarding its truthfulness. Teaching the theory as a scientific certainty is a massive hoax that has been perpetrated on students, beginning with America's very young children.

The theory of macroevolution is not only void of any real evidence, but it actually contradicts a large number of accepted laws of science. Because the theory is so weak, many scientists have turned to fraud and trickery in their effort to try to support it. Later in this chapter, a few of the more glaring examples will be exposed of evolutionists who have deliberately perpetrated fraud in an attempt to validate the theory. There are other scientists who actually admit they are unwilling to accept any evidence that contradicts the theory. Some of their names and quotes will also be found later in this chapter exposing why they stubbornly refuse to consider any truth that would dispel their pet hypothesis.

Before examining the many ways that the theory of macroevolution contradicts known laws of science, let's begin by scrutinizing the claim that all of life came into existence by mere random chance without design or meaning. To do so, let's consider the differences between things we know are created by nature and things we know are created by some form of intelligence. Things created by the nonintelligent forces of nature are random, often redundant, and sometimes complex. Things that are clearly created as a result of an intelligent design or a mind are highly specified and very complex. Below are some examples of each which should help clarify these differences.

Things Created by Nature	**Things Created by Intelligent Design**
Random cloud patterns	A message written in the sky that says, "Eat at Joe's Rib Shack on Main Street."
Redundant patterns in sand drifts	A sand castle with towers, widows, and a door
Complex patterns in raw marble	A marble statue of Napoleon Bonaparte
Random, redundant, and complex mountain peaks	Mount Rushmore

No thinking person would believe Mount Rushmore was created by the wind, rain, or other natural weather patterns, regardless of how many years it had been there. It is too specific and complex. It is obvious such a creation had to be designed and created by an intelligent mind.

If that is true for Mount Rushmore, imagine the specificity and complexity required to create a human being. Atheist Richard Dawkins, professor of zoology at Oxford University, stated a "single human cell contains a digitally coded database larger in information content than all 30 volumes of the *Encyclopedia Britannica* put together four times over .... Some species of the unjustly called "primitive" amoebas have as much information in their DNA as 1,000 *Encyclopedia Britannicas.*"[68] In addition, these 1,000 volumes of information are encoded on a compressed area less than one thousandth of an inch.

Even the coded DNA information in a single cell is too specific and complex to have been designed randomly by nature. Have you any idea how many times more specific and complex the coded DNA information is in a human being? If it is obvious that Mount Rushmore was created by an intelligent mind, it should be even more obvious that the DNA in humans had to have been created by an intelligent mind greater than the one that designed Mount Rushmore. Yet, evolutionary scientists expect us to believe it was all created through the random acts of nature though they have absolutely no published research to prove it.

Scientific laws

Not only does the theory of evolution fail the common sense test, it actually contradicts several established laws of science. Below is a list of just ten such laws:

1. Something cannot be formed from nothing.

Evolutionary theorists believe the universe began as a result of what is termed the Big Bang Theory. What caused this huge explosion to occur is unknown. Even more troubling is the fact scientists do not know what materials were involved in the explosion or where those materials (whatever they were) came from. In other words, evolutionary theory is at a total loss as to how matter first came into existence. Something had to be there before the "Big Bang" in order for something else to be created from it, because something cannot come from nothing. Something coming from nothing is a scientific impossibility, yet, that's what today's educators are teaching America's students happened.

2. Inorganic material cannot produce organic material.

In the 1960's, scientists were convinced a living organism could be created from non-living elements and began experimenting with amino acids to create some form of living material. These experiments are no longer being conducted because they concluded it could not be done due to the fact the coded DNA information required for life was impossible to create. Yet evolutionary scientists still believe it happened at one time eons ago. If it didn't happen, then the whole theory of evolution comes crashing down. Isn't it a bit too convenient that something which is known to be impossible took place anyway? To any unbiased observer such an event would have to be called a miracle.

3. Mutations never result in the creation of new DNA information

Evolutionists believe mutations are the answer to how evolution took place. The conundrum for this theory is that the mutation process *never* results in a mutation having any additional DNA information. In fact, just the opposite takes place – mutations *always* end up with equal or less genetic material. The results of mutation are defects, deformity, disease, and death but *never* new genetic material.

This is confirmed by the biophysicist Dr Lee Spetner, who taught at Johns Hopkins University:

> "In all the reading I've done in the life sciences' literature, I've never found a mutation that added information .... The NDT [neo-Darwinian theory] is supposed to explain how the information of life has been built up by evolution. The essential biological difference between a human and a bacterium is in the information they contain. All other biological differences

follow from that. The human genome has
much more information than does the
bacterial genome. Information cannot be
built up by mutations that lose it. A business
can't make money by losing it a little at a
time."[69]

Ernst Mayr, a famous evolutionist, thought
mutations would explain how evolution took place
but his own experiments with fruit flies proved just
the opposite! Despite years of experimenting with
genetic changes, the only changes that took place
were in the structure of the flies. He was able to
create fruit flies with more legs or wings, or with
parts protruding from places they aren't normally
attached to. But none of the changes resulted in the
formation of any new DNA information, which
would be required to form a new species. Nothing
evolved from his experiments other than fruit flies
and even they were left without any improvements
to their survival.

Seeing the results of his experiments, Ernst Mayr
tried to justify the results by saying evolution is an
"historical science" for which "laws and
experiments are inappropriate techniques" for trying
to prove the theory.[70] This explanation is dishonest,
however, since evolution is not only historical,
according to scientists, but continues to operate
today. Evidence for macroevolution should be
found now, as well as in history. The truth is it has
not been found at any time. No fruit fly, peppered
moth, or any other creature has ever formed a new

species through mutations and natural selection, and more and more top scientists are supporting that position.

Pierre Grasse, known as the greatest scientist in France, wrote, "No matter how numerous they may be, mutations do not produce any kind of evolution."[71] Professor Nils Heribert-Nilsson of Lund University has said, "There is no single instance where it can be maintained that any of the mutants studied has a higher vitality than the mother species." Nilsson added, "It is therefore, absolutely impossible to build a current evolution on mutations or on recombinations."[72]

Michael Pitman, former chemistry professor at Cambridge, confessed, "Neither observation nor controlled experiment has shown natural selection manipulating mutations so as to produce a new gene, hormone, enzyme system or organ."[73] The coholder of the 1945 Nobel Prize for developing penicillin, Sir Ernest Chain, called natural selection and chance mutations a "hypothesis based on no evidence and irreconcilable with the facts."[74]

If evolution is true, we should be able to observe and replicate gene mutations that produce new DNA information nearly everywhere we look, yet we cannot find any such mutations in nature, and scientists cannot produce a single example through experimentation. What we find instead are destructive mutations where the resulting material ends up with less genetic DNA information than was originally present. A great example of this was found in the recently discovered remains of what was thought to be an ancient but perfectly preserved octopus. The remains revealed this supposed ancient octopi actually had more genetic information than do modern octopi. Somewhere along the line they actually lost genetic DNA rather than gaining any. If anything, such evidence could be said to prove evolution in reverse.

4. The evolutionary process has taken place over billions of years.

This is not a proven law, but a theory that has to be true in order for evolution to be possible. The number of mutations involved in a single cell becoming a human being would require billions of years to transpire by sheer chance, even if mutations *could* produce additional DNA. If the mutations occurred randomly, as evolutionist claim, then the law of probability demands such a length of time. More on the probability of the evolutionary process taking place will be discussed under law number six.

Recent studies of the sun, however, have brought the age of life on earth into serious question. For example, John A. Eddy (Harvard-Smithsonian Center for Astrophysics and High Altitude Observatory in Boulder) and Aram A. Boornazian (a mathematician) have found evidence that the sun has been contracting about 0.1% per century . . . corresponding to a shrinkage rate of about 5 feet per hour."[75] If this is true, then by working backward we can determine that just 250,000 years ago, the sun would be twice its present diameter, making life on earth unsustainable. Even 100,000 years ago the sun would have been too large for the earth to sustain life of any kind.

Conversely, evolutionary theory claims life has been sustained on the earth for billions of years. If that is true, then the sun has remained relatively the same size during that entire period. How is that possible? How could something ablaze at the extreme temperature of the sun not burn up after all that time? Such an occurrence would be a greater wonder than the burning bush Moses encountered in Exodus chapter three. The fire from the burning bush only lasted a few minutes and the temperature of it was far less than the temperature of the sun. Thus, the non-consumption of the burning bush is far less of a miracle than is the sun burning for billions of years without losing any of its size.

The truth is the sun has been losing size. Serious measurements of the sun have been done for over 400 years and have found the decrease in size to be consistent over that entire time. The sun, 20 million years ago, would have been so large that it would have actually engulfed the earth. Thus, the earth itself (to say nothing of life on the planet) would have been completely consumed. This recent discovery of the sun's diminishing size means a single cell had to have become a human being in less than 100,000 years. Yet, that is mathematically impossible.

5. The Second Law of Thermodynamics

The first law of thermodynamics states that energy can be neither created nor destroyed. The second law of thermodynamics states that over time there is less and less usable energy. In other words, everything is deteriorating and becoming less complex. Things decay rather than build up, due to the decrease in creative (usable) energy. Once again, despite this established scientific law, evolutionary scientists claim the law worked in reverse for most of the earth's history as energy became more and more usable and things built up rather than decayed.

6. The Law of Probability

Evolutionary scientists also completely ignore the accepted law of probability. To illustrate this, consider the following probabilities:

a. The probability of a person playing 52 card pickup of picking the cards up in exact order (Ace through King) and by each suit (diamonds, hearts, clubs, and then spades) is 1/10 to the 68th power.

b. The probability of finding a particular atom in the universe is 1/10 to the 80th power.

c. Astronomers Fred Hoyle and Chandra Wickramasinghe used computers to calculate the probability that life would originate from non-life and found it to be 1/10 to the 40,000th power.[76]

An accepted rule in physics states that once the probability of an event occurring decreases below 1/10 to the 50th power, it has entered into the realm of the impossible. Apparently, the theory of evolution is exempt from the law of probability. The impossible can take place if it is needed to support your pet theory.

Prof. Harold Morowitz, former professor of molecular biophysics and biochemistry at Yale University and Robinson Professor in Biology and Natural Philosophy at George Mason University, estimated that the simplest theoretically conceivable living organism would have to possess a minimum of 124 different protein molecules. A rough estimate of the probability of all of these protein molecules to be formed by chance in a single chance happening would be 1/10 to the 8,060[th] power. In other words, the probabilities for the chance formation of a single working protein molecule or of a living cell are effectively zero. Imagine what the probabilities are for an even more complex organism.

Prof. Morowitz made a careful study of the energy content of living cells and of the building block molecules from which the cells are constructed. From this thermodynamic information he was able to calculate the probability that an ocean full of chemical "soup" containing the necessary amino acids and other building block molecules would react in a year to produce by chance just one copy of a simple living cell. He arrived at the astronomically small probability of 1/10 to the 340,000,000[th] power,[77] yet he still believed in abiogenesis, the spontaneous formation of the original living cells on the primeval earth.

Back in the 1970s Prof. Morowitz admitted in a public debate at a teachers' convention in Honolulu that in order to explain abiogenesis, it would be necessary to discover some new law of physics. At that time, he still believed in abiogenesis. Ten years later, however, he finally stated that in his opinion some intelligent creative power was necessary to explain the origin of life.

7. The Law of Irreducible Complexity

This law states that certain things have to have all of their parts in place in order to function. If you take any one part away it will no longer work. For example, a mouse trap must have every one of its parts, or it will not do what it was designed to do (i.e., catch mice). If you reduce it any further, it will no longer function. Such is the case for the DNA molecule, vision, and blood clotting, to name just a few. Conversely, you cannot simply add to existing things to create a working thing that is irreducibly complex. They have to be there in their entirety to begin with. This concept was first introduced by biochemist Michael J. Behe.[78]

The human eye, for example, couldn't possibly function without the cornea, iris, pupil, macula, vitreous humor, the rods and cones, the 100 million light-sensitive cells that send information to the brain through the one million fibers of the optic nerve, the brain itself, and the 100 billion nerve cells joined by some 240,000 miles of nerve fibers and the 100 trillion connections between nerve cells in the brain.

Gertrude Himmelfarb points out, "Since the eye is obviously of no use at all except in its final, complete form, how could natural selection have functioned in those initial stages of its evolution when the variations had no possible survival value?"[79] To imagine that vision's many essential parts could have developed over millions of years, while contributing nothing to survival until it all worked, is wishful thinking by those who will grasp at any idea to prop up a bankrupt theory.

Even certain amoebas are irreducibly complex and so had to have been formed in their entire completed state at the outset, or they would never have come into existence. Because an irreducibly complex organism could not have been created from any lesser form, molecular evolution is an impossibility.

8. Scientific theories must be based on evidence.

If animals have evolved continuously for billions of years, why are there no new species evolving today. Why would the evolution of creatures stop now? Why, in fact, do the fossil records lack evidence that such evolution ever took place at any time in history? Where are all the missing links?

When you consider the claim that man descended from some mutual link on the family tree as monkeys, one has to wonder why all the intermediate species are not still alive. If survival of the fittest is true, whatever beast preceded man should still be in existence, because monkeys still survive today. After all, monkeys are supposedly less fit than whatever evolved after them. If intermediate species did evolve after the monkey and before man, there should, at the very least, be hundreds of thousands (if not millions) of fossils of them in the uppermost layer of the earth. Not only are such creatures not alive today (as the theory of evolution would require), but there isn't even evidence they ever existed.

In 1980 *Newsweek* magazine reported the story of a scientific conference held in Chicago called "Macroevolution." During the conference, paleontologists told biologists that the fossil record does not, and never will, support the Darwinian theory of a smooth, continuous progress of life forms moving from simple to complex. Instead, the rocks show a pervasive pattern of gaps. New life forms appear suddenly with no transitional forms leading to them. Evolutionist Stephen Jay Gould called this discovery "the trade secret of paleontology."[80] Why is this information kept secret? What are scientists afraid of?

Johns Hopkins University Professor Steven Stanley of the Department of Earth and Planetary Sciences declared, "The known fossil record fails to document a single example of phyletic evolution accomplishing a major morphologic transition [a structural change relating to descent] and hence offers no evidence that the gradualistic model can be valid."[81]

In the same vein, Professor Heribert-Nilsson, director of the Botanical Institute at Lund University, Sweden, declared after forty years of study, "The fossil material is now so complete that the lack of transitional series cannot be explained as due to the scarcity of the material. The deficiencies are real; they will never be filled. The true situation is that those fossils have not been found which were expected. Just where new branches are supposed to fork off from the main stem it has been impossible to find the connecting types."[82]

Scientific theories are constructed from evidence obtained from observation and experimental research. This is not true, however, for the theory of evolution. Not only is there no fossil evidence to be observed, but no actual occurrences. No one has ever observed molecular evolution taking place, nor has any scientific research been published to show how molecular evolution could occur naturally. This is astonishing to say the least. The theory is taught as true to students everywhere, yet there is no experimental evidence for it.

As absurd as it sounds, what the theory of evolution asks us to believe is that animals were able to adapt to their surroundings by giving birth to progeny that were entirely different from their parents. It's like saying because a carpenter has to work hard to survive, his children will be born with calluses on their fingers. If mammals with lungs needed to breathe underwater to survive, would their offspring be born with gills? Are we asked to believe that hippos might have spent so much time in the water that they eventually developed into whales by mere mutation? And lizards with scales spent so much time jumping from trees to trees they eventually became birds with feathers?

These are the kinds of fantasies usually reserved for creating children's bedtime stories. Instead, they are taught as truths without an ounce of evidence and are written in science textbooks as scientific facts.

9. Scientific theories are based on duplicated experiments which consistently obtain the same results.

To be considered valid, any experiment demonstrating a theory to be true must have the same results when the experiment is duplicated. Indeed, regardless of the number of times the experiment is repeated, the results must remain the same. This has not been done for the theory of molecular (or macro) evolution, however, because there has never been even one successful experiment to reproduce.

10.Scientists do not deny, tamper with, or falsify evidence in order to uphold a theory.

A number of scientists who believe in evolutionary theory have deliberately attempted to deceive the public with false information, beginning with Darwin himself, right up to the current day. Hoaxes like the "Nutcracker Man" and "Lucy" have been committed by unscrupulous scientists from the time the theory of evolution was first introduced.

A German scientist, Ernst Heackel, was a very influential proponent of the evolutionary position as well as an advocate of atheism. He attempted to portray himself as an ethical proponent of atheism; history, however, shows he was a very deceitful individual. The March 9, 1907 edition of the *NY Times* referred to Ernst Haeckel as the "celebrated Darwinian and founder of the Association for the Propagation of Ethical Atheism." What the *NY Times* did not report was the many frauds Haeckel had perpetrated on the public. In one case, Haeckel made drawings of the embryos of various species showing how very similar they were in design. His contention was that different animals all start out looking almost identical, thus showing the evolutionary connection between them all.[83] The problem with his drawings was the fact they were not at all like the embryos they were supposed to depict. He had deliberately distorted their actual shapes, sizes, attachments, and appearances in order to convince people they were similar to each other. Even though every embryologist who ever lived knew his drawings were phony, they still ended up in science books as evidence for the theory of evolution. Sadly, his fallacious drawings still appear in school textbooks today.

I remember in high school seeing pictures of light colored and dark colored moths resting on tree trunks. According to scientist Bernard Kettlewell, the light colored moths turned into dark colored moths as a result of evolution.[84] This theory was based on the fact the tree trunks had changed colors due to a new factory in the area that was spewing coal ash into the air. The moths had to change colors (evolve) for survival, as they protected themselves from being eaten by birds by blending in with the color of the tree bark. Because the tree trunks became dark, the moths had to do the same in order to survive (continue to camouflage themselves while resting on the tree bark).

Apart from the obvious fact the moths were still moths and only their color had changed, there was another fact Kettlewell deliberately withheld. The moths did not (neither before nor after the factory was operating) land on the tree trunks. They only landed in the leaves of the branches of the trees and not on the bark of the trees. Kettlewell had glued lifeless moths to the trunks of the trees before taking the pictures, because they could not be photographed there in their natural state since they never landed there. It was a sham. Like Haeckel's fraudulent embryo drawings, Kettlewell's phony moth photos are still used in textbooks today as evidence for evolution.

Charles Dawson, a follower of Darwin, claimed he discovered a Piltdown skull in a gravel pit. He also discovered an elephant bone there that had been carved into a shape similar to a cricket bat. This discovery supposedly proved that the Piltdown Man used tools. Dawson was blessed with remarkably good luck in finding a great number of fossils, so much so, that he became known as the wizard of Sussex.[85] After his death in 1916, however, no more Piltdown fossils were ever found anywhere in the area despite ongoing searches.

The Piltdown fraud was finally uncovered by geologist Kenneth Oakley, anatomist Wilfrid Le Gros Clark, and anthropologist Joseph Weiner in 1953.[86] They found the impressive cranium actually belonged to a modern human and the jawbone belonged to an orangutan or a chimpanzee. All were stained to look old and to match. The teeth had also been filed down to make them look older than they were. What no one had detected for forty years was now plain for everyone to see, and Piltdown Man was moved from the evolutionary hall of fame to the hall of shame.

The annals of history are replete with examples of scientists concealing, tampering with, and falsifying evidence in an attempt to justify the theory of evolution. It appears these scientists believe the theory needs to be bolstered by fraud because it cannot stand on its own merit. Fraud needs to be used to successfully convince the masses of the theory of evolution, because the scientific evidence is not there.

Not all believe

Further dishonesty by evolutionists can be found in the unsubstantiated claims they make with great bravado, but without shame. Atheist, Richard Dawkins, for example, once wrote, "No reputable scientist refuses to accept evolution."[87] Apparently, Dawkins believes any scientist who disagrees with him on this subject is not reputable. In 2010, almost a thousand major scientists, all with doctorates, signed a document that made the following statement: "We are skeptical of claims for the ability of random mutation and natural selection to account for the complexity of life."[88] These scientists are experts in such fields as medicine, biology, geology, anthropology, zoology, physics, and genetics holding doctoral degrees from universities such as Rutgers, MIT, Baylor, Oxford, Dartmouth, Tulane, Columbia, Cornell, Princeton, Purdue, Indiana, Yale, Duke, Stanford, Cambridge, Temple, and Berkeley. According to Dawkins, none of these scientists are reputable.

What is even more outrageous is that evolutionists call everyone (including the brilliant scientists just mentioned) ignorant for not believing in macroevolution. Despite the fact their theory cannot be shown to be true experimentally, lacks the fossil evidence to show it to be true, uniformly contradicts known laws of science, and has historically been propped up with false statements and outright fraud, we are asked to believe evolutionists when they tell us their theory is true.

If the evidence doesn't support the theory, then the theory should be abandoned, but it has not been. Why not? It seems unlikely the evolutionists are not current with the latest findings. It would seem more likely there is a bias that blinds them to the evidence or lack thereof.

Admittedly, some atheistic evolutionists are more honest than others. For example, Ernst Mayr was honest enough to state outright, "Darwinism rejects all supernatural phenomena and causations."[89] In other words, Darwinism is not open to evidence if it points to intelligent design.

Scott C. Todd, a professor in the Department of Biology at Kansas State University, proclaimed, "Even if all the data point to an intelligent designer, such a hypothesis is excluded from science because it is not naturalistic."[90] Todd is saying truth is to be ignored if it doesn't fit into naturalistic theory. Such a position results in a belief in evolution regardless of the evidence, not because of it.

Richard Lewontin of Harvard has stated:

"We take the side of science in spite of the patent absurdity of some of its constructs. . . in spite of the tolerance of the scientific community for unsubstantiated commitment to materialism. . . .we are forced by our *a priori* adherence to material causes to create an apparatus of investigation and set of concepts that produce material explanations, no matter how counterintuitive, no matter how mystifying to the uninitiated.

Moreover, that materialism is absolute, for we cannot allow a Divine Foot in the door."[91]

Speaking of the trust students naturally place in their highly educated college professors, physicist Mark Singham candidly admitted:

"And I use that trust to effectively brainwash them. . .our teaching methods are primarily those of propaganda. We appeal it without demonstration to evidence that supports our position. We only introduce arguments and evidence that supports the currently accepted theories and omit or gloss over any evidence to the contrary."[92]

As far as the twentieth century is concerned, the leading evolutionist is generally considered to be Sir Julian Huxley, primary architect of modern neoDarwinism. Huxley called evolution a "religion without revelation." He argued passionately that we must change "our pattern of religious thought from a God-centered to an evolution-centered pattern."[93] He went on to say, "the God hypothesis . . . is becoming an intellectual and moral burden on our thought." Therefore, he concluded that "we must construct something to take its place."[94]

Atheistic evolutionists seek truth only as long as it does not result in the conclusion that an intelligent designer exists. All evidence for God must be ignored, suppressed, or discredited. According to their own admissions, alternative theories of how life began must be created regardless of how untenable they may be. If they refuse to follow truth wherever it leads, perhaps Richard Dawkins had it backwards. It would appear it is the atheistic evolutionists that are not reputable scientists.

When the beautiful black sand beach on the Big Island of Hawaii was overrun by lava from the volcano, scientists said it would be a long time before anyone would ever see another black sand beach. They estimated it took years to produce such a beach. A few months later, however, a new black sand beach had been created by the very volcano that had wiped out the previous one. Apparently, when the hot lava flows into the cold ocean water it can quickly break up into tiny particles as it cools, thus creating black sand. This sand can then wash up on shore and in very little time create a new black beach. Imagine the chagrin of the scientists who emphatically stated it would take several years.

Likewise, the faces of scientists today who teach the theory of macroevolution as fact should be red with embarrassment. The massive amount of recent and not-so-recent evidence that the theory is totally fraudulent should leave them nonplussed. Unfortunately, most scientists are not deterred and continue to shamelessly extol the theory as fact. This theory is now so engrained into the fabric of our society, especially in the minds of America's youth, that it is unlikely any amount of evidence disputing the theory will make a difference. NeoMarxists are banking on the fact that exposure to the truth will not change anyone's mind. As previously stated, the theory of evolution greatly serves the goals of socialists by eliminating the need for a belief in a creator God while, at the same time, devaluing human life.

CHAPTER 9: KEEPING THE PEOPLE IGNORANT

During the early days of America, every child read and learned from the Bible. It was taught daily in the public schools. Today the average student has never even seen a Bible in school, to say nothing of having read one. Even though our judicial system was built on Judeo-Christian values taken from the Bible, the average student has no idea what information is contained in the greatest book ever written. It is doubtful that even 1% have read it from cover to cover.

The biblical ignorance of current students was perfectly illustrated on April 4, 2020, on an episode of Jeopardy's College Championship. Only the brightest of students are picked to participate in this quiz show. One young man from Northwestern University made it all the way to the semi-finals. He demonstrated a great deal of knowledge on just about every subject presented except one – the Bible. One of the answers he was asked to respond to was "After he returns, in Luke 15, his Dad says, 'Bring hither the fatted calf, and kill it, and let us be merry.'" The student responded by saying, "Who is Cain?" Not only did he not know the story of the Prodigal Son, but it appears he thought the New Testament book of Luke is where the story of Cain and Abel is found.

This college student is not unique in his ignorance of the Bible. Ask almost any college student a question such as, "Who wrote the

Gospels?" and you will receive a blank stare. They will be clueless. They may not even know how many Gospels there are to say nothing of having read one. They have not studied or even read the book that is annually purchased by more people than any other book ever written in all the world. That is because they have been duped into believing that there is no God and the Bible is not credible or relevant. After all, if the Bible contained important truths that students should learn, it would be taught in school. Because it is actually banned from school, students conclude that it is not worth reading.

Once again, those seeking to instill socialism have succeeded in accomplishing one of their major goals. Their efforts have resulted in a nation that is almost completely biblically illiterate. The nation will remain biblically illiterate as long as Bibles are kept out of public schools and the Bibles that are outside schools continue to collect dust on home and library bookshelves.

It would come as a major shock to most students (and many adults as well) to learn that there is more than ample evidence to demonstrate that what is written in the Bible is completely credible and relevant. So much so, that many (including former atheists) who have undertaken the task of disproving the Bible have, after close examination, become believers instead. Later in this chapter, several reasons will be given for judging the Bible to be a credible source of information.

Faith without evidence is dangerous.

Socialists want you to think that atheism is based on reason while belief in God is based on blind faith in irrational superstitions or archaic traditions that have been passed down from previous generations. But such atheists are wrong. While some who say they believe in God demonstrate little reasoning ability, it does not follow that all believers in God are irrational. For the majority, a belief in God is based on far more than blind faith. It is based on evidence and personal experience that leads one to a reasonable conclusion.

To believe something is true without any evidence whatsoever is irrational and foolish or is the result of a mental imbalance. Such beliefs can lead to harm for the believer. If a person believes a chair is behind him, for example, without any evidence a chair is really there, the person is either ridiculously naive or is crazy. If the person is nonetheless convinced the chair exists and sits down, the person ends up crashing to the floor. Such blind faith is not smart, or even sane, and is definitely not safe.

On the other hand, when one sits on a chair that is clearly visible, faith is still involved. Even though there is physical evidence the chair exists, there is no guarantee the chair will hold up under the person's weight. One sits down believing the chair will not break apart based on faith. Such faith is not irrational or the result of mental instability, but it is based on previous experience and evidence. Chairs have held people up in the past, and unless the chair looks defective in some way, all the evidence would lead one to believe he can safely sit in the chair. If one is able to sit comfortably in the chair, then his faith was well placed. If not, he will feel he has been deceived into believing something that was not true. In either case, it was a reasonable to trust the chair to hold up, based on the knowledge the person had of his own weight and the size and construction of the chair. It is not irrational to trust a chair to hold up when you sit in it, but it does require faith.

Without faith, man would be unable to do anything he does every day. He would not venture out of his house since that too requires faith. Even though you cannot be absolutely sure you will not have an accident when you leave home, you leave anyway based on faith. The evidence shows the odds of you being in an accident are low enough to warrant your stepping out. Your safety, however, cannot be 100% assured, but staying home for the rest of your life is not a very good option. In truth, you could even have an accident at home.

So, faith is required in every aspect of life. Without it, man could not function, but faith must be based on solid evidence and relevant experience. Faith should not be mere wishful thinking or irrational speculation. This is especially true when it comes to a belief in God. Such a belief should be based on evidence. Furthermore, no one can authoritatively declare there is no God if they have not examined the evidence. This is true for everything that exists.

God is not dead.

For example, most readers of this book have no knowledge of my brother, Frank. Not only do you, dear reader, know nothing about what he is like, you don't even know if he exists. Because you have never met my brother, you may conclude that he doesn't exist and that I am not being truthful when I claim he does.

Regardless of what you conclude, however, I personally know he exists because I have seen evidence of his existence many times. I have experienced for myself his big bear hug. Others have the option to accept or not accept the reality of my brother based on my word. If you don't believe I am telling the truth or, perhaps, I am mentally deranged, you will decide he does not exist. If you believe I am credible, you will accept my word for his reality. Either way you decide, it will have no impact on the absolute truth of his existence. If you ultimately decide he does not exist, then you are basing that belief on total ignorance.

You may, of course, decide you are uncertain of his existence because you have never had any firsthand knowledge of him. What you cannot do, however, is definitively know that he does not exist because he may exist outside your sphere of knowledge (see the "Knowledge Diagram" in Chapter Two). In order to be absolutely certain Frank does not exist, you must believe there is no knowledge beyond what you know. Such a conclusion is the pinnacle of arrogance. You are saying, "I possess ultimate knowledge" and "I know that all those who claim to have met Frank are wrong while I am right." Could there be anything more prideful?

This kind of arrogant thinking is what makes up the atheist's philosophy. Unlike the agnostic, who questions the existence of God, the atheist boldly asserts that he knows there is no God simply because he is ignorant of any personal knowledge of Him. Such a ridiculous position would be equivalent to a scientist categorically claiming there are no living organisms anywhere in the universe other than those on the earth. Such a claim would be foolish because the scientist has never visited or examined every planet in every galaxy. Because the scientist knows he lacks universal knowledge, he would never make such a claim.

Suppose the scientist was able to visit other planets and discovered a living organism, say on Mars. The organism's existence would be an absolute truth regardless of anyone's thoughts, feelings, or beliefs about it. Truth is not relative simply because I question its veracity.

Ignorance is no excuse.

There is no excuse for being ignorant of reality when knowledge of it can be found through investigation. One evening, when I was a boy, my father asked me to answer a science question. He told me the answer to the question would be an obvious one. He asked me which was heavier – a pound of feathers or a pound of steel. Obviously, steel is much heavier than feathers, so I gave him the obvious answer – steel. I was wrong, of course, because a pound is a pound the world around, regardless of how much material is required to reach the weight of one pound. The obvious answer to my dad's question was, "They are the exact same weight."

I had considered only part of the information my father had given me and not all of it. I had taken the words feathers and steel and concluded the steel had to be the heavier of the two. I had not taken the other facts into consideration because I was sure I had sufficient facts to know the obvious answer. Similarly, if you have never encountered God or seen a miracle, then you might conclude that you have sufficient information to believe there is no God. This is, of course, precisely what atheistic socialists want you to conclude. The last thing atheistic socialists want you to do is to investigate the evidence. They want to keep America ignorant of God. That is why they have convinced educators to remove Bibles from schools.

Atheists know that most people become Christians as a result of Bible knowledge. It is for that reason they portray the Bible as being full of inaccuracies, contradictions, and myths in an effort to discourage anyone from reading it. The only thing that would stand in the way of them accomplishing their goal would be for people to discover that the Bible was accurate, contained no contradictions and presented real truth. How do we know the Bible is all that? Below are half a dozen reasons to believe the Bible is completely trustworthy.

The Bible is historically accurate.

While revisionists have attempted to rewrite much of the Bible, its earliest manuscripts contain a precise history of what took place during the times in which the writers recorded what they did. One of the ways scholars determine the accuracy of an historical account is by comparing it with other accepted historical writings from the same time period. Based on all the other information we have from the various time periods described in the Bible, it is not hyperbole to say the Bible is completely trustworthy in its recording of history. It can be relied upon to give very detailed accounts of what took place at the times being described, including what countries existed, who was king or ruler over them, what customs people practiced, and any number of other historical facts. Nothing has been found showing the Bible recorded something that contradicts known facts of history.

Another way, scholars determine the accuracy of an historical account is by examining the trustworthiness of the authors. Whether the historians are writing about what happened to George Washington, Napoleon, Hitler, or Jesus, they must be considered honest reporters before any confidence is placed in the truth of what they have written.

So why should we believe the writers of the Bible? One reason is because they were eyewitnesses to the occurrences:

- Luke (the author of Luke and Acts), for example, claimed he recorded the testimony of eyewitnesses who were there at the time of Christ and saw what happened (Luke 1:1-4; Acts 1:1). He wrote that Peter said, "This Jesus has God raised up, whereof we all are witnesses" (Acts 2:32). Later, Peter also said, "We are witnesses of all things which he did both in the land of the Jews, and in Jerusalem; whom they slew and hanged on a tree: Him God raised up the third day, and showed him openly; not to all the people, but unto witnesses chosen before of God, even to us, who did eat and drink with him after he rose from the dead" (Acts 10:39-41).

- Luke joined Paul's team in Troas (Acts 16:8-10), and the remainder of Acts is an eyewitness account. - Peter himself wrote, "For we have not followed cunningly devised fables, when we made known unto you the power and coming of our Lord Jesus Christ, but were eyewitnesses of his majesty. For he received from God the Father honour and glory, when there came such a voice to him from the excellent glory, 'This is my beloved Son, in whom I am well pleased.' And this voice which came from heaven we heard, when we were with him in the holy mount" (2 Peter 1:16-18).

-     John, the Apostle, also tells us he was a witness to Jesus along with many others. He wrote, "That which we have seen and heard declare we unto you." (I John 1:3)

What happened was recorded by those who were there at the time including fishermen like John, a doctor named Luke, Peter, and Paul, a one-time hater of Christians. There were also historians whose words were not recorded in the Bible that give testimony to the life of Jesus.

Atheists and skeptics have suggested the writers were either delusional or just plain dishonest. If they were delusional, there are several questions that have to be asked. How is it possible so many people hallucinated the same thing at different times? Why didn't a single contemporary ever make such a claim about these witnesses? How is it possible none of the writers showed any signs normally associated with individuals not dealing in reality? All the writers were lucid and clear in their writings. Where is there found any evidence to suggest they were delusional?

If the writers were sane but dishonest in their reporting, what was their motive? It certainly wasn't for personal glory. They portrayed themselves as ignorant, lacking in faith, sinful, and often inept. If they were lying about the events that took place, it seems likely they would also lie about themselves and record how good they were as disciples. The fact they didn't gives indication they were being honest in what they wrote.

The ultimate test of their reliability is found in their willingness to die for the risen Lord they wrote about. If the whole story were just a fictitious tale, why would they be willing to be tortured for it? They must have believed it was true. Otherwise, at least one of them would have "spilled the beans" especially just before he was to be beheaded. What's the point of being a martyr for what you know is a hoax?

Furthermore, there were other historical writers of the time who were not followers of either the Jewish religion or of Christianity who recorded the existence of Jesus. There are more than 6,000 manuscripts (including secular ones) that record the existence of a person named Jesus. In fact, there is more evidence for the existence of Jesus than there is for any other individual in all of antiquity. There are very few manuscripts, for example, that indicate there once was a man named Plato, yet we have no trouble believing he existed. Why then (with the superior evidence available for Christ's existence) do people claim Jesus was a myth or a fable? The problem of acceptance isn't found in any inaccuracies of the historical records. The inability of people to trust the records is primarily due to their unwillingness to do so. People do not want to believe the Biblical record despite the abundance of evidence. Their doubts are dishonest doubts.

The Bible is prophetically accurate.

In addition to its historical accuracy, the Bible is also true prophetically. No prophecy given in the Bible has ever turned out to be wrong. This alone should make a believer out of the most adamant skeptic. Even though there is no doubt all the Old Testament prophecies were written hundreds of years before the New Testament fulfillment of them, every one of them turned out to be correct. To be 100 percent accurate in predicting future events is more than just improbable, it is impossible apart from an omniscient God. Compare 100% to the success rate of secular predictions.

A study of psychics in 1975 and observed until 1981 showed that of the seventy-two predictions, only six were fulfilled in any way. Two of these were vague and two others were hardly surprising – the U.S. and the Soviet Union would remain leading powers, and there would be no world wars. The People's Almanac (1976) did a study of predictions of twenty-five top psychics. The results: Of the total seventy-two predictions, sixty-six (92%) were totally wrong. An accuracy rate around 8 percent could easily be explained by chance and general knowledge of circumstances. In 1993 the psychics missed every major unexpected news story, including Michael Jordan's retirement, the Midwest floods, and the Israel-PLO peace treaty. Among the false prophecies were that the Queen of England would become a nun and Kathie Lee Gifford would replace Jay Leno as host of "The Tonight Show" (*Charlotte Observer*, 12/30/93).

Old Testament prophets, on the other hand, had to be 100% accurate, because they were stoned if any of their prophecies failed (Deuteronomy 18:20). Of the hundreds of Old Testament prophecies, not a single error has been found. The odds of even a half dozen predictions happening exactly as foretold is beyond comprehension. Neither the ability of man nor simple chance can account for such perfection in knowing the future. Note, for example, the dates of the following prophecies concerning Jesus and then the dates of their New Testament fulfillments.

PROPHECY	B.C. DATE/ REFERENCE(S)	A.D. DATE/ REFERENCE(S)
Be born in Bethlehem	700 B.C./Micah 5:2	60-65A.D./Matthew 2:1-6 *circa* 60/Luke 2:1-20
Be born of a virgin	740-680/Isaiah 7:14	60-65/ Matt. 1:18-25 *circa* 60/Luke 1:26-38
Be a prophet like Moses	1405/Deuteronomy 18:15, 18, 19	85-90/John 7:40
Enter Jerusalem in triumph	520-518/Zechariah 9:9	60-65/Matt. 21:1-9 85-90/John12:12-16
Be rejected by his own people	740-680/Isaiah 53:1,3 *circa* 1000/ Psalm 118:22	60-65/Matt. 26:3, 4 85-90/John 12:37-43 61-70/(Luke) Acts 4:1-12
Be betrayed by one of his followers	*circa* 1000/ Psalm 41:9	60-65/Matt. 26:14-16; 26: 47-50 *circa* 60/Luke 22:19-23
Be tried and condemned	740-680/Isaiah 53:8	60-65/Matthew 27:1, 2 *circa* 60/Luke 23:1-25
Be silent before his accusers	740-680/Isaiah 53:7	60-65/Matt. 27:12-14 55-65/Mark15:3-4 *circa* 60/Luke 23:8-10
Be stuck and spat upon by his enemies	740-680/Isaiah 50:6	60-65/Matt. 26:67; 27:30 55-65/Mark 14:65
Be mocked and taunted	*circa* 1000/ Psalm 22:7, 8	60-65/Matt. 27:39-44 *circa* 60/Luke 23:11, 35
Die by crucifixion	*circa* 1000/Psalm Psalm 22:14, 16, 17	60-65/Matt. 27:31 55-65/Mark 15:20, 25
Suffer with criminals and pray for his enemies	740-680/Isaiah 53:12	60-65/Matt. 27:38 55-65/Mark 15:27, 28 *circa* 60/Luke 23:32-34

Be given vinegar and gall	*circa* 1000/	60-65/Matt. 27:34
	Psalm 69:21	85-90/John 19:28-30
Lots cast for his	*circa* 1000/	60-65/Matt. 27:35
garments	Psalm 22:18	85-90/John 19:23, 24
No bones ever broken	1445-1405/	85-90/John 19:31-36
	Exodus 12:46	
Die as a sacrifice for sin	740-680/Isaiah 53:5,	85-90/John 1:29; 11:49-52
	6, 8, 10, 11, 12	
Rise from the dead	*circa* 1000/	60-65/Matt. 28:1-10
	Psalm 16:10	61-70/Luke 24:1-7;
		Acts 2:22-32
Be at the right hand	*circa* 1000/	55-60/Mark 16:19
of God	Psalm 110:1	*circa* 60/Luke 24:50, 51

Atheists and doubters, of course, try to argue that the New Testament writers simply wrote the history of Jesus in a way that would fulfill the earlier prophecies. Such a futile attempt to avoid the obvious fails on a number of counts. First, there was no reason for the writers to do that. If anything, the incentive was not to do so. The religious leaders not only rejected the idea that Jesus was the predicted Messiah, but they ridiculed, imprisoned, and even tortured those who thought He was. Even the disciples were unsure as to whether or not Jesus was who He said He was. They would not have tried to convince themselves of His authenticity by falsifying the facts. Just the opposite occurred. The facts were what convinced them He was, indeed, the Messiah.

Additionally, if they had created false narratives about Jesus, no one living at the time would have believed them. They would have been easily exposed and laughed at, yet, thousands of people became followers of Christ based on what the disciples said about Him.

Furthermore, there is no record of anyone producing evidence that disproves what Jesus did or that the disciples made up stories about Christ to fit every single prophecy given about the Messiah. There were even non-believers who recorded that Jesus did what the disciples claimed He did. Finally, there are too many other prophecies in the Bible that cannot be explained away by suggesting later writers corrupted their recorded history in order to make the prophecies come true. For example, the Jews were told they would be disbursed from their homeland into all the other countries of the world (Ezekiel 22:15). According to the experts, Ezekiel was written between 593-560 B.C. It wasn't until 70 A.D. (hundreds of years after the prediction was made) that this prophecy came true. Historians of all stripes recorded this to be true. The Bible also predicted the Jews would ultimately return to their homeland. This prophecy was made by several Old Testament writers including Amos (Amos 9:14-15), written in 755 B.C. Prior to 1948 A.D., no one even imagined the Jews would come together from the far corners of the globe and form the new country of Israel, yet, that is exactly what happened over 2,000 years after it was predicted in the Bible. There are people still living today who can verify that is what occurred.

Only one book from all antiquity – the Bible – has ever made hundreds of prophecies that were 100% accurate. How is this possible if it is simply the writings of mere mortals? Only God knows the future with absolute certainty. Only He could be flawless in making so many predictions.

The Bible is archeologically accurate.

A third way the Bible is accurate is archeologically. As in the two previous areas, the Bible has been found to be 100% reliable here as well. There has never been an archeological discovery that showed the Bible to be wrong. World-class archaeologists from around the world, including Millar Burrows of Yale, William F. Albright, and Sir William Ramsey have all studied the biblical records and concluded the same thing.

Professor F. F. Bruce noted that "archaeology has confirmed the New Testament record."[95]

Archaeologist Nelson Glueck has boldly asserted, "It may be stated categorically that no archaeological discovery has ever controverted a biblical reference. Scores of archaeological findings have been made which confirm in clear outline or exact detail historical statements in the Bible."[96]

Dr. Joseph P. Free stated, "Archaeology has confirmed countless passages which have been rejected by critics as unhistorical or contradictory to known facts. Yet archaeological discoveries have shown that these critical charges are wrong and that the Bible is trustworthy in the very statements which have been set aside as untrustworthy. We do not know of any cases where the Bible has been proved wrong."[97]

To this day, archeologists continue to discover findings that validate the Biblical record.

The Bible is philosophically sound.

The Bible is also sound philosophically. The Bible presents a worldview that is both thorough and consistent. It explains how the universe began and how time will end, provides a moral code for both individuals and societies, and offers a transcendent purpose for living. It answers all of life's important questions and explains what constitutes the ideal. No other worldview is as complete and void of contradiction.

Much needs to be dealt with on this topic, but rather than taking a great deal of space here in this book, I will defer such a discussion and recommend a book that does a brilliant and thorough job of comparing the various world views. Most importantly, the book clearly demonstrates why the Christian worldview is far superior to any other. The book leaves little doubt as to the soundness of Biblical truth. I encourage everyone to read "Unshakable Foundations" by Norman Geisler and Peter Bocchino.

The Bible is experientially accurate.

From a personal standpoint, the most important way the Bible is found to be trustworthy is through experience. For centuries, men and women have discovered experientially that the Bible is totally reliable in every way. In it they have found the truth that has led them to the hope, love, and guidance they had previously been unable to find anywhere else. Many were living lives in futility and despair until they began believing in and following the Bible. Afterwards, they report finding satisfaction never before realized. They testify to discovering a life more abundant than they could have ever imagined. Are these millions of people all delusional? If so, I am one of them. Like so many others, I have not only found the Scriptures to be true, but God to be faithful in answering my prayers. He has even performed miracles in order to meet my needs. The most amazing miracle He performed took place during my college years.

In the summer of 1970, after the spring planting season was over, I was laid off at the local Agway store where I had been working while attending college. There simply wasn't enough work to justify keeping me on, despite the fact my wife and I had a newborn baby and no other source of income. To make matters worse, the rent was due and we didn't have any money to pay it. While our small apartment wasn't much, it was all we had. The $70 monthly charge in 1970 might as well have been $10 million as far as our ability to pay was concerned. We had a mountain of financial troubles at that time.

The rent was due Monday, and it was now Sunday evening. We had no known source of relief available to us except one. We decided to pray together for a miracle from God. We had nowhere else to turn, so together we knelt down beside the living room couch and prayed for $70. It was a very emotional time for us, and we both found ourselves crying as we got up from our knees. As we sat back down on the couch, still wiping the tears from our eyes, there was a knock on the door. It was late and so we looked at each other wondering who would be visiting us at such an hour.

The visitor introduced himself as Tom Thompson. He asked me if my name was Gil, and if I remembered meeting Tom at a Bible study weeks earlier. I said I was indeed Gil, but I was sorry to say I couldn't remember meeting Tom. Tom said that was okay. The important thing was that Tom had remembered me. Tom explained how he was a donor to a number of national and international Christian organizations, including Billy Graham, World Vision, and others. But lately he sensed God was telling him he needed to give more locally. So, while continuing to give to these other organizations, he was praying about where he should give more money right here in his own home town of Wellsville, New York. He went on to explain that every time he prayed about where he should give and to whom, my name came up. He said, "I pray and I think of you." I expressed surprise, especially because I didn't even remember meeting Tom.

Again, Tom said that didn't matter because God was more concerned that Tom remember me. He said, "I have no idea what your financial situation is right now, Gil, but I feel God wants me to give you this tonight," and he handed me a check for $70. It was *exactly* what we had prayed for, *exactly* what we needed to pay our rent the next day. Needless to say, this started my wife and me crying again. As we explained our story to Tom, tears welled up in his eyes. He knew then he had indeed heard God correctly and had obediently responded to His leading.

Throughout our life together, my wife and I have experienced God's miraculous provision on numerous occasions. Multitudes of others say the same thing. We certainly are not unique in knowing the Lord is a miracle worker and wonderful provider. The Bible is true when it says, "God shall supply all your need according to his riches" (Philippians 4:19).

Atheists may contend that Tom's arrival was simply a coincidence. I find that harder to believe than to believe in God. To suggest it was simply luck that Tom arrived exactly when he did (right after we had prayed and just before the rent was due), chose me out of all the people in town he could have given money to (a population of thousands), gave me exactly the amount I was praying for ($70), and remembered my name after meeting me only once (and without even knowing I had a financial need) stretches the laws of probability beyond any honest measure.

When I told this story to a friend of mine, he suggested I write up the story and submit it to *Guidepost Magazine* for publication. I did and received a letter from the magazine's editor stating they receive so many of these types of letters they could not use any more including mine. What he was saying to me was that my extraordinary experience was commonplace. So many people had similar stories to tell that he had an overabundance of them. I now tell people who suggest such miraculous happenings are merely coincidental they may be right, but I find the more I pray, the more these coincidences happen.

The Bible is scientifically accurate.

This will no doubt surprise some, but the Bible has also been found to be 100% accurate scientifically on everything it has to say about scientific matters. Granted, when it tells of God's intervention into the laws of nature (i.e., He often performs miracles such as walking on water), He defies the normal laws found in creation. That is not the same, however, as making statements about the laws of nature themselves. It is understandable that God can change the laws of nature, given the fact He is the one who created them in the first place. He certainly has the right and the power to change them if He should choose to do so. If He could not, He would not be the sovereign God. The point is, apart from these special interventions of God, nothing stated in the Bible about nature has been proven to be contrary to the known laws of science. There are, of course, statements that people claim contradict science, but they do not. They only contradict the "theories" of science (theories which cannot be proven). The most obvious one is the theory of macroevolution discussed in the previous chapter.

Those who dare to question any of these theories are said to be people who do not believe in science. This is a misnomer, however, because it is not scientific facts that are being questioned but the unsubstantiated hypotheses that scientists make. Nevertheless, the majority of people in America today have been convinced by radical neo-Marxists that Bible-believing Christians who reject any of the unsubstantiated postulates made by scientists are ignorant religious fanatics possessing unscientific minds. As was mentioned earlier, many of the world's greatest scientists, including many today, believe in God despite the common notion that all scientists hold to a completely non-theistic naturalistic worldview. There are Christian astronomers, physicists, chemists, and even biologists, with high IQ's and extensive educational backgrounds. Some of them are currently making extraordinary new discoveries in their chosen fields. The assumption that atheists are smarter than theists is just that – an assumption.

At the present time, it is fashionable for skeptics to consider themselves brilliant simply because they question anything spiritual. Dallas Willard, professor of philosophy at the University of Southern California, makes the following observation: "We live in a culture that has, for centuries now, cultivated the idea that the *skeptical* person is always smarter than one who believes.

You can be almost as stupid as a cabbage, as long as you *doubt*."[98]

I once heard a very arrogant individual say, "Christians are so ignorant they still believe in a flat earth." Actually, had people read and believed the Bible they would have discovered the earth was round long before Christopher Columbus sailed the ocean blue. Isaiah 40:22, which was written thousands of years before 1492, informs us that God "sitteth upon the circle of the earth." It was ignorant scientists and not the scientifically accurate writers of the Bible who taught the earth was flat. God informed man the earth was round long before any humans figured it out. This is true of many scientific facts found in the Bible, though they were written thousands of years ago. It is the scientists who are found to be wrong over and over again as new and more revealing discoveries are made that disprove their older theories.

In summary, the Bible is completely trustworthy historically, prophetically, archeologically, philosophically, experientially, and scientifically. Despite its accuracy, however, the Bible is to be considered a book of mere fairy tales by those who do not want Americans to believe in God. It is not enough that the nation has been moved far away from its Christian heritage, it must now become completely secular in order to usher in the new "utopia" of democratic socialism.

EPILOGUE

How can America survive when truth is being eradicated, history is being revised, divisions are being sown between races and political parties, laws are being passed that will bankrupt the nation, God has been removed from society, and free speech is being silenced? The answer is, America will *not* survive unless things change. The only way to keep America from becoming a socialist country is for citizens to get involved in fighting against this counter-culture movement. This will not be simple or easy.

It will require citizens to investigate what is being taught in their children's schools. This means asking students, teachers, and board members tough questions. It means joining the PTA, attending meetings, and speaking up. It means finding out how school board members vote on school policies and curriculum. It may necessitate campaigning for and electing the right board members. It involves educating your neighbors, family, and friends about the issues.

It is critical that politicians are elected at every level who seek to preserve the constitution and who represent America's traditional values. This includes electing a President who will not give in to the radical left's demands.

Most importantly, it requires teaching our children the truth about absolutes, history, race relations, the constitution, morality, and God, especially about God.

President John F. Kennedy gave our nation a powerful challenge when he said, "My fellow Americans: ask not what your country can do for you – ask what you can do for your country." The idea of serving the country is an anathema to those who wish to replace America. Their desire is to abolish capitalism because it isn't giving them everything they want. If you believe you are entitled to something you are not being given, you have a choice as to how you respond to your perceived mistreatment. Anarchists have decided to riot, destroy property, violently attack, and even kill, to obtain their demands.

Why do they think such extreme behavior is justified? Aleksandr Solzhenitsyn, who became a political prisoner after telling the truth about the evil of Marxism, said this, "It is not because the truth is too difficult to see that we make mistakes. It may even lie on the surface; but we make mistakes because the easiest and most comfortable course for us is to seek insight where it accords with our emotions – especially selfish ones." In other words, if it feels good – believe it. We tend to decide what is true based on our emotions rather than on logic and facts. As a result, extremists are not open to rational thought. They are convinced they are right and will not be swayed by an opposing view, even if it more accurately represents the truth. In their opinion, the end justifies the means.

So, are these anarchists motivated by altruism or selfishness? Actually, it is neither. There are basically only three motivators to anyone's actions.

Fear

The first is *Fear*. Whether it is fear of failure, fear of punishment, fear of looking bad, fear of losing a job or a friend, many people live their entire lives out of fear. They get up every morning (or perhaps evening) and go to work for fear of being fired if they don't. They don't rob a bank for fear of being caught and sent to jail. They fail to speak their minds for fear of ridicule. Whatever actions they take or not take are decided based on their fear of the consequences.

Fear keeps them from taking the risk of trying something new or of making any major changes to their lives. Fear results in a lifestyle that may be safe, but is dull, provincial, and lacking in any exciting adventure. Those who go through life motivated by fear are the unhappiest of all people. The question that looms before them when deciding what to do is, "What can I *lose*?"

Hope

The second motivator is *hope*. Social workers spend a great deal of time trying to instill hope in the hopeless. Hope is certainly better than fear, but hope as a sole motivator for living does not result in lasting happiness either.

These people get up in the morning and go to work in the hope of earning enough money to pay their bills, getting a promotion and/or raise (climbing the corporate ladder), providing their family with a sense of financial security, or perhaps in the hope of purchasing a particular desired object, such as a house, car, or dream vacation trip. These people do what they do in the hope of getting things they long for. The question for people motivated by hope is "what can I *gain*?"

Violent anarchists appear to be motivated by anger and hate. But individuals with such attitudes are really just motivated by another form of hope. Whether it is the hope of getting revenge for wrongs done to them, the hope of destroying what makes them angry, or the hope of punishing those they believe are evil, their actions are motivated by hope. Driven by anger and hate, people do things they hope will result in a particular desired end.

Love

The final motivator, the greatest of all, is *love*. The question asked by people motivated by love is "what can I *give*?"

People motivated by love live their lives meeting the needs of others rather than being concerned about making sure their own needs are met. They look for opportunities to serve rather than worrying about whether they are getting their fair share. They even love their enemies.

To understand what motivates a person, listen to the questions he or she asks before they make a decision.

Fear asks – What can I lose?
Hope asks – What can I gain?
Love asks – What can I give?

Are you completely satisfied with life?

The happiest person of the three will be the one motivated by love. In contrast, those motivated by anything other than love will live their entire lives dissatisfied, because they will never gain enough to bring them lasting contentment. They will always be wanting something more.

This dissatisfaction is evident in those who hate and curse conservatives, who burn down buildings, who violently attack police officers, and who destroy whatever and whomever stands in the way of them getting their demands met. They are unaware of the fact that even if they should get their way, they will remain unsatisfied. Only a life motivated by love is grounded in a contentment that is lasting.

When will I find love?

Everyone needs love. Everyone searches for love. Unfortunately, we never have that need met completely by other people, because they too are in need of love as much as we are. They too are hoping to find perfect unconditional love from us, but we are incapable of providing it. No one ever receives the love they need from other people, because no one is able to give it. If we cannot give it, then we can't expect to ever receive it. People are simply incapable of giving to others what they themselves desperately seek.

So where does one turn to have this great need met? The need is met only by the One who created the need within us in the first place. He is the only one capable of giving us the perfect love we long for. Americans need to turn back to God and ask Him to place His love in our hearts. But God cannot fill with love what is already full of other things. We must empty our hearts of all self-interest. It's hard to imagine a world where every person cares more about others than they do themselves. That may be why heaven will be heaven. Here on earth, such a world would require a miracle never before seen.

God tells us in 2 Chronicles 7:14, "If my people, who are called by my name, will humble themselves, and pray, and seek my face, and turn from their wicked ways; then will I hear from heaven, and will forgive their sin, and will heal their land." If, and only if, our nation returns to its early Christian foundation will it ever again be "a shining city on a hill." May God bless America.

NOTES

Chapter 1:

1. National Intelligence Council, "Assessing Russian Activities and Intentions in Recent US Elections", ICA 2017-01D, January 6, 2017.

2. The 116th Congress, 1st session Senate report ii6-xx. Report of the Select Committee on Intelligence United States Senate on Russian active measures campaigns and interference in the 2016 U.S. election, volume 1: Russian efforts against election infrastructure.

3. Samantha Bradshaw, University of Oxford and Philip N. Howard, University of Oxford, *Troops, Trolls and Troublemakers: A Global Inventory of Organized Social Media Manipulation*, "Computational Propaganda Research Project", Working paper no. 2017.12.

4. Walter E. Williams, article entitled "Socialism's Past." Published on March 18, 2020.

5. Ilya Somin, article entitled "Perils of "Democratic Socialism," The Volokh Conspiracy. Printed on June 5, 2019.

6. John Adam, article entitled: "Pilgrim Lesson: Spreading Wealth Leads to Pooled Poverty." Printed November 23, 2011.

7. Dr. Thomas Sowell, article entitled, "Socialism for the Uninformed." Printed May 31, 2016.

8. Jason Mattera, article entitled "Utopians must destroy the family." Printed on January 19, 2012.

9. Andrew Scott, article printed June 5, 2010.

Chapter 3:

10.From the private journal of Secretary of State
Adams (1820).

11.Journals of the Continental Congress
(Washington: Government Printing Office,
1905), Vol. III, pp. 350-351, November 11,
1775.

12.Journals of the Continental Congress (1907),
Vol. VII, pp. 72-73, January 30, 1777.

13.Journals of the Continental Congress (1909),
Vol. XV, pp. 1181-1182, October 16, 1779.

14.Journals of the Continental Congress (1928),
Vol. XXVII, pp. 659-660, December 3, 1784.

15.Journals of the Continental Congress (1905),
Vol. III, p. 433, December 16, 1775.

16.Journals of the Continental Congress (1906),
Vol. IV, p. 267, April 10, 1776.

17.George Washington, *The Writings of George
Washington*, John C. Fitzpatrick, editor
(Washington: U. S. Government Printing
Office, 1936), Vol. XV, p. 55, from his speech
to the Delaware Indian Chiefs on May 12, 1779.

18.John Hancock, "A Brief," dated June 20, 1788.

19.Library of Congress, Papers of the Continental
Congress, No. 28, folio 203.

20.Journals of Congress, pages 468-469. September
1782. Found at the Library of Congress at
https://www.loc.gov/exhibits/religion/vc006473.jpg

21.*Ratification by the States*, Volume VI:
Massachusetts, No. 3.

22.Daniel Webster, *Mr. Webster's speech in defence
of the Christian ministry, and in favor of*

The religious instruction of the young. Delivered in the Supreme Court of the United States, February 10, 1844, in the case of Stephen Girard's will. Washington: Printed by Gales and Seaton, 1844.

23. Jon A. Shields, article entitled "The Disappearing Conservative Professor," National Affairs, Fall 2018.

24. Peter Schweizer, *Makers and Takers* (New York: Doubleday, 2008), p. 157.

25. Ibid., p. 162.

26. Ibid., p. 171.

Chapter 4:

27. Statista Research Department, Jul 1, 2020.

28. Sharyl Attkisson, "Media Mistakes in the Trump Era: The Definitive List*," Untouchable Subjects. Fearless, Nonpartisan Reporting.* Posted June 23, 2020.

29. *Reconstruction: America's Unfinished Revolution, 1863–1877.* (New York: Harper & Row, 1988).

30. History.com Editors, July 7, 2020. URL: https://www.history.com/topics/reconstruction/kukl ux-klan

31. W. E. Burghardt Du Bois, *Black Reconstruction in America: 1860–1880*, (New York: Oxford University Press, 2007), pp. 680–81.

32. *Wikipedia*, July 2, 2020.

Chapter 5:

33. James V. Fee, "Book reviews," *Today's Speech*,

January 1973.

34. The Village of Skokie, Appellee v. National Socialist Party of America et al., Appellants. No. 49769. Supreme Court of Illinois. Opinion filed January 27, 1978.

35. https://www.conservapedia.com/Censorship, October 17, 2019.

Chapter 6:

36. Guy Sorman, article entitled "Climate Science's Myth-Buster." Published winter edition 2019.

37. Ian Plimer, article entitled, "97% Of Scientists Agree on Nothing." Published by The Global Warming Policy Forum on January 17, 2019.

38. https://nsidc.org/data/seaice_index.

39. http://ocean.dmi.dk/arctic/icecover.uk.php.

40. https://electroverse.net/more-record-gains-for-greenland-ice-sheet.

41. https://www.newscientist.com/article/mg207277 94-400-kilimanjaros-vanishing-ice-due-to-treefelling.

42. https://www.newsweek.com/volcanic-activitymelting-antarctic-glacier-below-998522.

43. This quote is often attributed to Mark Twain, but there's no evidence that the author actually wrote or spoke the phrase.

44. Guy Sorman, "Climate Science's Myth-Buster," Winter 2019. https://www.city-journal.org/global-warming.

45. Andrew Orlowski, "Climategate 2.0: Fresh trove

of embarrassing emails."
https://www.theregister.co.uk/2011/11/23/climatega
te_2_first_look.
46.Guy Sorman, "Climate Science's Myth-Buster,"
Winter 2019.
https://www.city-journal.org/global-warming.

Chapter 7:
47.Frederick Neitzche, *Supermen*, "Thus Spoke
Zarathustra," Prologue 3, (1983-1985),
translation by Walter Kaufmann.
48.Bertrand Russell, *Why I Am Not a Christian and
other essays on religion and related subjects*
(New York: Simon & Schuster, 1957), p. 62.
49.Alfred J. Ayer,"A Critique of Ethics." *Ethical
Theory: An Anthology*. Ed. Russ Shafer-
Landau, (Oxford: Blackwell Publishing Ltd,
2007), pp. 18-24.
50.Jean-Paul Sartre, "Existentialism and Ethics."
Moral Education. Barry I. Chazan and Jonasa
F. Soltis, Eds. (New York: Teachers College
Press, Columbia University, 1973), reprinted
from *Existentialism*, (New York: The
Philosophical Library, 1947), pp. 11-61.
51.Larry Taunton, "Richard Dawkins: The Atheist
Evangelist," *by Faith*, Issue Number 18,
December 1, 2007.
52.Seneca the Younger, *On Anger*, 1.15.2.
53.Jeff Jacoby, "Created by God to Be Good",
Globe.com, November 14, 2010.

Notes 54-66 are taken from

"http://www.conservapedia.com/Atheism and morality."

54. Joe Carter, "The Dangerous Mind of Peter Singer," *First Things First*, June 22, 2011.
55. Justin Smith, "The Basis of a Christian Worldview," *Creation Ministries International*, November 22, 2006.
56. Christopher Hitchens vs. William Lane Craig, Biola University, April 4, 2009.
57. Richard Warden, "Atheist Achilles Heels: Objective Morality and Sacred Life," August, 10, 2012.
58. RSS feed - Lacrimae Rerum, blog of Skatje Myers, blog article Zoophilia, October 2, 2007.
59. Kyle Butt vs Dan Barker debate, "The Butt/Barker Debate: Does the God of the Bible Exist?" (Montgomery, AL: Apologetics Press, 2009). http://www.apologeticspress.org/APContent.aspx?category=12&article=2333.
60. Jeffrey Lord, "When Nancy Met Harry," *The American Spectator Special Report*, October 5, 2006.
61. Steven Baldwin, "Child Molestation and the Homosexual Movement," *Regent University Law Review*, Vol.14:267, p. 272. http://www.mega.nu/ampp/baldwin pedophilia homosexuality.pdf.
62. Matt C. Abbott, "The Mind of a Pederast,"

Renew America, August 22, 2010.
http://www.renewamerica.com/columns/abbott/100
822.

63.Samuel R. Delaney, *About writing: seven essays, four letters, and five interviews*, p.36. 64.Carl Freedman, "Conversations with Samuel R. Delany," (University Press of Mississippi, 2009), p. 143.

65.Zygmund Dobbs, *Keynes at Harvard: Economic Deception as a Political Credo*, A Veritas Study, 2009.
http://www.keynesatharvard.org/book/KeynesatHa r vard-ch09.html.

66.Ibid.

67.Organization for Economic Cooperation and Development, OECD, PISA (Program for Student Assessment) 2003 database.

Chapter 8:

68.Richard Dawkins, *The Blind Watchmaker*, (New York: W. W. Norton, 1986), p. 115.

69.Dr Lee Spetner, *Not by Chance*, (Brooklyn, NY: The Judaica Press, Inc.), p. 131–132, 138, 143. See review in Creation 20(1):50–51, December 1997–February 1998.

70.Ernst Mayr, "Darwin's Influence on Modern Thought," Scientific American, (vol. 283, July 2000), p. 83.

71.Grasse, Pierre-Paul, *Evolution of Living Organisms*, (New York: Academic Press, 1977), p. 88.

72.Professor Nils Heribert-Nilsson, *Synthetische*

Artbildung [Synthetic Speciation] (1953),
p. 1157.

73. Michael Pitman, *Adam and Evolution*, (London: Rider & Co; First Edition, 1984) *pp. 67-68.*

74. Sir Ernest E. Chain, "Social Responsibility and the Scientist in Modern Western Society" (Robert Waley Cohen memorial lecture, 1970).

75. Gloria B. Lubkin, *Physics Today,* V. 32, No. 9, 1979 and Russell Akridge, Ph. D., 1980. "The Sun Is Shrinking," *Acts & Facts.* 9 (4).

76. Fred Hoyle and N. Chandra Wickramasinghe, *Evolution from Space*, (Aldine House, 33 Welbeck Street, London W1M 8LX: J.M. Dent & Sons, 1981), pp. 24, 30, 31, 148, 150.

77. Harold J. Morowitz, *Energy Flow in Biology*, (New York: Academic Press, 1968), p.84.

78. Michael J. Behe, *Darwin's Black Box: The Biochemical Challenge to Evolution*, (New York: The Free Press, 1996).

79. Gertrude Himmelfarb, *Darwin and the Darwinian Revolution*, (Garden City, New York: Doubleday, 1959) pp. 320-338.

80. Stephen Jay Gould, "Evolution's Erratic Pace," *Natural History*, vol. 86 (May 1987), p. 14.

81. Steven M. Stanley, *Macroevolution: Pattern and Process*, (San Francisco: W. H. Freeman, 1979), p. 39.

82. N. Heribert-Nilsson, *Synthetische Artbuilding* (*The Synthetic Origin of Species*) (1953), 1212.

83. Ernst Heackel, *Natürliche Schöpfungsgeschichte* (Berlin, 1968).

84. H.B.D. Kettlewell, "Selection experiments on

industrial melanism in the Lepidoptera," *Heredity*, 9:323342, 1955.

85. Miles Russell, (2003), *Piltdown Man: The Secret Life of Charles Dawson*, Tempus, Stroud, pp. 157–71.

86. "End as a Man," *Time Magazine*. November 30, 1953.

Notes 87-94 are taken from Henry Morris, Ph.D., 2001, *Evolution Is Religion--Not Science, Acts & Facts*, 30 (2).

87. Richard Dawkins, *The Greatest Show on Earth: The Evidence for Evolution*, (New York: Free Press a division of Simon & Schuster, Inc., 2009), p.9. (Originally published in Great Britain by Bantam Press an imprint of Transworld Publishers).

88. Don Boys, "Almost a Thousand Major Scientists Dissent from Darwin!" *Canada Free Press* (Sunday, May 2, 2010). *A Scientific Dissent from Darwinism* is a statement first issued in 2001 by the Discovery Institute.

89. Ernst Mayr, "Darwin's Influence on Modern Thought," *Scientific American* (vol. 283, July 2000), p. 83.

90. Scott C. Todd, "A View from Kansas on the Evolution Debates," *Nature* (vol. 401. September 30, 1999), p. 423.

91. Richard Lewontin, Review of *The Demon-Haunted World*, by Carl Sagan. In *New York Review of Books*, January 9, 1997.

92.Mark Singham, "Teaching and Propaganda,"
    Physics Today (vol. 53, June 2000), p.54.
93.Julian Huxley, *Essays of a Humanist*, (New
    York: Harper and Row, 1964), p. 222.
94.Ibid.

Chapter 9:
95.F. F. Bruce, "Archaeological Confirmation of the
    New Testament." *Revelation and the Bible*,
    Edited by Carl Henry. (Grand Rapids: Baker
    Book House, 1969), p. 331.
96.Dr. Nelson Glueck, *Rivers in the Desert*, (New
    York: Farrar, Strous and Cudahy, 1959), p. 136.
97.Dr. Joseph P. Free, *Archaeology and Bible
    History*, (Wheaton, IL: Scripture Press, 1969),
    p.1.
98.Dallas Willard, *Hearing God: Developing a
    Conversational Relationship with God*,
    (Illinois: InterVarsity Press, 1999), p. 218.